Painting Patterns
for Home Decorators

This design is in three parts which may be used separately; combined or repeated in different ways for decorating trays, drawer fronts and many other articles. The background of the object may be white, cream, ivory, blue, gray or black. The design is transferred as described in the chapter on this subject. The outlines are then filled in with white, American vermilion, medium chrome yellow, light leaf green and bottle green as shown in full color on page 43. The chapter on color formulas tells how each subtle color variation may be mixed without buying extra tubes of paint.

Painting Patterns
for Home Decorators

by

RUTH WYETH SPEARS

Book 1

BONANZA BOOKS
NEW YORK

Manufactured in United States of America

CONTENTS

ACTUAL-SIZE TRACING PATTERNS

FOREWORD

IF YOU can trace the outlines of patterns and fill in spaces with color, you can paint the attractive things shown in this book. In time you will be making freehand flourishes with the greatest of ease, but you do not have to do it that way in the beginning. If you can cook by a recipe or mix a simple formula, you can follow the rules given here for mixing colors —a full range of them, bright and gay or subtle and soft. The pattern tells you where to use each one, and as you fill them in, the design comes to life under your hand.

You will find much the same kind of pleasure in painting with a pattern to guide you as you might find in following the notes of a simple musical melody to produce rhythm and harmony. At first you will be conscious of what your hands are doing. With practice, technique will become second nature, and you will interpret designs more freely. If you would paint in the gay and carefree manner that is so typical of all folk art or so-called peasant art, remember that the peasant artist has used a brush almost from infancy, and certain motifs in painting are as familiar to him as the folk songs that his mother sang as she rocked his cradle.

Many of the designs given here remind me of ballads and folk songs, and as I have worked on the drawings and directions for them, I have liked thinking of this book being used in much the same way that an old-fashioned songbook might be used. There is something in it for every member of the family. There are old themes and new and modern adaptations of things that have a familiar air. In a way these patterns link the present with the past in a kind of continuity, but they all are planned for use in the homes of today.

Some of the motifs in these designs are very old. Conventionalized flowers, hearts, scrolls, birds, and figures are typical of the folk art designs of every country of Europe. Many of them originally came from the Orient. In the handcrafts of the colonial period in this country, bird and flower designs used by the North American Indians were often copied. The cave man decorated his dwelling with crude drawings of the animals he saw. He had no designs of any other place or period to copy.

Today, when we copy the painting designs of the early Dutch settlers in Pennsylvania, a little of the flavor of our own times creeps in. Our designs are not exactly like theirs. Neither were their designs exactly like those that they copied from the pieces of furniture and other things that they brought with them to the New World. They improvised a little and experimented with ideas of their own. They applied old designs to new uses just as we do. They used the kinds of paints and materials that were available. If the results were good, others in the community copied them. Everybody copied everybody else, and yet they evolved something distinctive and individual to the time and the region.

And if we turn from this simple craft type of painting to the more naturalistic designs that were used in New England in the early eighteen hundreds to decorate chairs and trays and other household articles, we find that many of the most typical motifs of that time were borrowed from other countries and other periods just as we borrow and adapt designs today. The rose and the ivy designs that we like to use also were popular then. Thousands of years ago the Persians used the rose in decorative designs. Wherever you turn in the study of decoration, from ancient Greece down to the present, the ivy theme is likely to show up. You come to think of it as an old friend and watch for different versions and applications. The same is true with many of the other basic motifs in the design given here.

Once you have actually painted one of these traditional motifs you will remember it as you would remember a familiar bit of melody. It will never be quite the same twice, and yet you will always recognize it. Your appreciation will be keener for having made your own little rendition of it. If this book helps you to do that, it will actually have served the same purpose that a book of simple tunes might serve for one who likes to sing rather than paint. Yet I am glad that this is a book of painting designs instead of songs. A song floats off into space when it is sung. When you paint something that you like, you have it to use and enjoy, to give away or even to sell. If you do not like it, you can always paint the design out and start over again.

IN A DECORATING SCHEME

Morning-glories on a painted frame around the window at the right repeat the blue of an upholstered chair and the rug. This window treatment is more dramatic than flowered draperies would be and much easier to care for.

Below at the left, a chest of drawers with heavily antiqued ivory background and green decoration is an accent piece in a living room furnished in mahogany and upholstered furniture. The lamp and decorated box pick up and repeat red and gold tones used throughout the room.

At the right below, a gay rag rug and chairs painted different colors repeat tones in the painted designs on the doors of a cupboard so simple in design that it easily could be made at home.

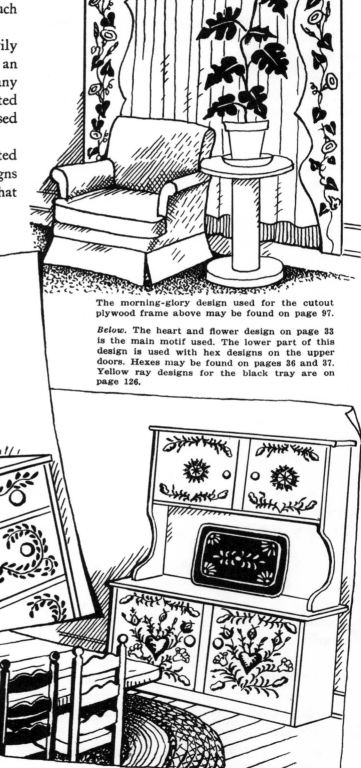

The morning-glory design used for the cutout plywood frame above may be found on page 97.

Below. The heart and flower design on page 33 is the main motif used. The lower part of this design is used with hex designs on the upper doors. Hexes may be found on pages 36 and 37. Yellow ray designs for the black tray are on page 126.

Above. Designs from pages 53, 68, and 87 are used for the lamp and box. Leaf sprays on page 61 are used to decorate the chest of drawers.

THE THINGS YOU PAINT

How to harmonize them
in a room decorating scheme

IF YOU GO into any shop which specializes in gifts and smart accessories for the home, you will find that many of the choicest things are hand painted. Decorators are also using painted furniture in rooms of almost every type. A third way that painted designs are being used is for wall decorations in panels, borders, or designs painted on the wall to make an effective setting for some piece of furniture.

Study the illustrations given here, and you will see how painting designs may be skillfully woven into the decoration of any room. You will see that individual things are decorated in designs of the right scale for their size. The design fills the space in a pleasing way. There are no spotty effects. Cupboard doors are decorated to make interesting panels —never in little motifs with too much bare space around them. Pieces of furniture do not break out in a rash of small designs, but spaces are filled adequately and with some regard to general contours and construction. Where a number of designs are used in one room they are in harmony though not necessarily all alike. Each design plays its own part. They do not all compete for the center of the stage.

Generally the best results are obtained by using designs that are in harmony with the feeling or spirit of the room—gay simple motifs for informal rooms, quaint designs for rooms with a quaint period feeling, designs a little more sophisticated for formal rooms. Yet even as I write this, I think of any number of rooms where designs in direct contrast to the general feeling of the other furnishings have been used with wonderful effect. Contrast is often needed to give a room life. Most of us have come to realize that any room that slavishly follows the decoration of any period, place, or way of thinking is extremely dull. It is as though the people who lived there had never traveled, had no new ideas, or had never received a gift or bequest from someone who lived in another period.

Color can be a great harmonizer in assembling things of different types. Small painted objects may add as much life and interest when properly placed in a room as costly accessories made of rare materials.

Painted furniture often is used to emphasize more important pieces. A beautifully decorated desk, chest of drawers, or a table, an occasional chair or a pair of side chairs may be used in a room with the finest mahogany or even in a modern room furnished mainly in bleached wood. Such pieces play a supporting role. They should never be allowed to steal the show. The trick is in using the right overtone and surface glaze to subdue their coloring as explained here under Final Finishes.

But painted designs do not always have to play a secondary part in a decorating scheme. It is when they are the star attraction that you begin to get effects that will lift the most humdrum furnishings out of drabness. If your room is not furnished with fine mahogany, but with an ill-assorted lot of odds and ends, paint can be your salvation. Color is yours for the asking. You can paint any piece of furniture, walls, ceiling, or floor any color you want. You can use as much or as little pattern or design as is needed to lend interest. You can use surface finishes to give richness, depth, or brilliance according to the effect desired. Some pieces of furniture may be made to fade into the background, others may be brought forward, all with the clever use of paint. And here is something that I hope you will not forget. When you paint things yourself, treat them as though they have worth. Make them count in your decorating plan.

If you want to use painting designs as the outstanding feature of a really beautiful room that is restful without being monotonous, do not, under any circumstances, give the decoration of all parts of the room equal value. Choose a focus point and turn the spotlight on it. Let some one gayly decorated piece of furniture dominate the scene. You may have to do a little carpenter work in order to produce a piece of the right scale for the purpose. When this is done, paint the piece with a background color that harmonizes with other colors in the room, and then decorate it with a design of lively interest in colors that may be repeated and echoed throughout the room. Other less important pieces of furniture then

Little borders painted on rich background colors make fascinating
containers and flower holders of ordinary boxes and cans, and a
bird on a vine turns a tin tray into a thing of beauty.

may be decorated in such a way that they pick up the theme established by this central piece, much as a chorus might follow a song theme to support a star in the leading role.

As you read the descriptions with the illustrations given here, you will see how the painting patterns in this book may be used in this flexible manner to produce the effects you want. There are main motifs and supplementary motifs and many suggestions for combining and adapting them for a great variety of purposes. Some of the applications you will be able to copy for a purpose somewhat similar or for the same use as the one shown. You will also find that the designs suggest many other uses and that they may serve as basic motifs to which you may add many ideas of your own.

MATERIALS FOR PAINTING

What to use and how
for everything from tin to fabric

A FEW TUBES of paint, two or three brushes, a little turpentine and clear varnish, an old plate for a palette, and some clean rags are all the equipment that you actually need to start decorating with painting designs. However, if you decorate a wide variety of objects, there are a few extras that will help you with special problems. The things you need to know are described here under separate headings so that you can refer to them quickly for reference. You will also find it worth while to read through the entire list in the beginning so that you will have a general idea of what to do when the occasion arises.

Brushes. For painting designs, you will need round brushes of fine hair that tapers smoothly to a point. Red sable water-color brushes are best. These brushes are purchased according to the width at the tip of the metal ferrule that holds the hairs. For most of the work, you will need a brush about one-quarter inch wide. A brush about one-eighth inch wide also is needed, and if there are fine lines in the design, one-sixteenth inch wide will be required. If you do much painting, time is saved by having one of these brushes for each main color in the design; then you do not have to rinse the brush each time you change colors. For painting backgrounds of small objects, a one-inch wide flat bristle brush will be useful.

Oil paints for designs. Artists' tube oil colors are used generally for painting these designs. For most work, these should be thinned as you work by dipping your brush in a small jar containing a mixture of two parts turpentine and one part clear white waterproof varnish. Special thinning mixtures are used with these paints for painting on glass, tin, oilcloth, and fabrics of various sorts as described under separate headings. The colors required and formulas for mixing them are fully outlined under Paints and How to Mix Them.

Linseed oil. For this kind of painting, oil is not needed for thinning the paint, and any paint that has much oil in it is unsatisfactory because it runs as you work. It is possible to let such paint stand until the oil comes to the top, then pour it off and use the pure pigment in the bottom of the can for painting decorations or for stenciling. Boiled linseed oil is generally purer than the raw type. It is used with powdered pumice to rub a final coat of varnish to give a beautiful soft finish.

Turpentine. When you use oil paints, turpentine is absolutely essential for your mixing medium and for rinsing brushes. Be sure to get the best quality.

Varnish. The best quality of clear uncolored waterproof varnish is needed to use in the mixing medium for painting designs to give body to artists' oil colors. It is also invaluable for a final finish after the decorating is completed and dry, and is mixed with turpentine and paint in preparing a surface overtone or antique finish.

Japan drier. As the name suggests, this liquid speeds the drying time of paint. It also has an adhesive quality which makes paints to which it is added adhere to smooth surfaces such as metal and glass. Enamels for interior use have considerable drier in them. Use drier sparingly in paint to decorate anything that is to stand outdoors as it causes the paint to dry out and rub off when exposed to the weather. Buy the smallest container of japan drier and follow the directions that come with it. Remember that in painting designs you are working with very small quantities of paint. A drop or two of drier will go a long way.

Mixing medium. In painting designs, the paint is thinned as you work by dipping your brush in a small jar of mixing medium consisting of two parts turpentine and one part clear white waterproof varnish. If the design calls for one color painted over another and you wish to speed the drying of the first color before applying the second, add a little japan drier to this mixture. Some artists always include a dash of drier, but it is not essential in most work. Also keep a small open jar of clear turpentine at hand for rinsing brushes as you work.

Palette and mixing jars. It is always best to use a palette when painting designs, but it does not have to be a regular artists' palette. An old plate, a piece of window glass, or even the pages of a coated paper magazine will do. Set up your palette with colors squeezed from the tubes or with thick paint that you have mixed. Most artists are particular about having colors always in the same position along the upper edge of the palette—usually starting with white and the light colors at the upper right and shading to the darker ones toward the left. This leaves the lower part of the palette free for mixing and blending colors. A little paint will go a long way in decorating. Half a spoonful is enough of most colors to have on your palette at one time. If you wish to mix more of a color than this amount, keep it in a small tightly covered jar and take out a little at a time. Keep your palette clean. A messy palette is often the cause of muddy painting.

Palette knife. A flexible palette knife with a blade about two and a half inches long is useful for mixing paints and for cleaning your palette. This is not an absolutely essential bit of equipment, but if you do much painting you will want one. Palette knives in various sizes may be obtained at any store that sells artists' materials.

Clean rags. You will need plenty of soft clean rags for drying brushes and for wiping surfaces so that they will be free of dust. Cleaning tissue will do for drying small brushes, but nothing really takes the place of rags.

Decorating tin and other metals. Tin trays and even pans and cooking utensils may be turned into articles that are both beautiful and useful if decorated attractively. Old flatirons may be decorated for book ends. A metal coffeepot and teapot may make a watering can for house plants. The list is endless. As a rule, if the metal is clean and free from rust and grease, any good gloss or semigloss enamel will stick to it for a background. But do not forget that even new metal generally has an oily coating. Always wipe it with a rag dipped in turpentine to remove this. If the design is to be painted directly on the metal without a painted background, use artists' tube oil colors mixed with clear waterproof varnish and a tiny bit of japan drier. Small things of tin painted all over have a richer appearance and wear indefinitely if finished either with glossy or mat-finish waterproof varnish.

Painting on glass or glazed pottery. Beautiful effects are obtained by painting flowers and other designs on clear glass. Glazed pottery jugs, jars, and dishes may also be decorated effectively. Pure high-gloss enamel is sometimes used for this purpose. There is also a prepared paint for glass obtainable at artists' supply stores. Ordinary tube oil paints mixed with clear varnish and a dash of japan drier will also adhere to glass and glazed surfaces and may be used for a long time without wearing off. If you want to paint a background on glass or a glazed article, use enamel of the color desired or tint white enamel with tube oil paint. Another method is to varnish the piece first and then apply paint in the usual way.

Painting flowerpots and porous pottery. Enamel usually sticks fairly well to flowerpots and other porous pottery. If you wish to paint a design directly on the pottery, use tube oil colors mixed with clear waterproof varnish. A priming coat of clear varnish often is used before painting this type of pottery.

Painting on oilcloth. Table mats, children's bibs, and many other things of gayly decorated oilcloth are attractive. Pure enamel or white enamel tinted with tube oil color may be used for the decorating, or tube oil colors mixed with clear varnish and a little japan drier may be used.

Painting lamp shades. Old parchment paper lamp shades may be given a new lease on life by painting them inside and out with semigloss enamel. Use ivory or cream inside and a darker color outside. Simple borders top and bottom or larger designs may then be painted on this background. Even the old edge braid may be freshened with paint. A new parchment paper lamp shade may be decorated with ordinary tube oil paint. If you wish to make the shade, use three-ply kid-finish Bristol board. Oil this by rubbing it lightly with a soft cloth moistened with linseed oil. Fit a piece of newspaper or wrapping paper over the wire frame you wish to use, and then use it for a pattern to cut the parchment paper. Sew or glue the parchment paper to the frame after the decorating design has been traced on it. Paint the design with tube oil paint. After the design is dry, clear varnish may be applied if desired.

Outdoor furniture. Decorated furniture for the yard is quaint and gay in bright designs of hearts, flowers, or scrolls. Such pieces should always be given a protective coat of good heat- and water-resistant spar varnish after the design is thoroughly dry.

Decorating with crayons. Wax crayons may

be used to decorate unfinished wood and other dull surfaces. Varnishing the piece after it is decorated will fix the crayon so that it may be washed. Care must be used in applying the first coat of varnish so that the design will not be blurred. Pat it on lightly with a soft cloth, if necessary. After this first light coat is dry, a second heavier coat may be added with a brush. The final coat may be rubbed to take away the high gloss, if desired. Chalk or pastel crayons also may be used for decorating. They give a beautiful soft effect for wall treatments. A special fixative for pastel crayons and an inexpensive spray for applying it may be purchased at artists' supply stores. Neither wax nor chalk crayon will work on a surface that has been painted with oil paint. A water paint background makes a good working base for either.

Decorating with water paints. Tempera colors in tubes or show-card colors in jars are easy to use for painting designs on almost any surface that is not too glossy or that has not been oiled. They are not satisfactory for glass or glazed pottery and cannot be used on a high-gloss enamel background. However, if the enamel is dulled slightly by rubbing with fine sandpaper, these water paints will adhere. A design painted with them may be made waterproof by varnishing over it after the paint is dry. In applying the varnish, care must be used to avoid rubbing and smearing the paint.

Fabric paint. If you wish to paint designs on cloth for curtains, table mats, or similar articles, it is possible to buy fabric paint at stores that sell artists' materials. This paint may be washed or dry-cleaned without fading. Oil paints thinned with turpentine also may be used for this purpose. After the paint is dry, the colors may be fixed so that they are fade resistant by placing a cloth dampened with vinegar over the design and pressing with a warm iron.

Gold paint. Most of the old-fashioned trays and chairs decorated in gold designs on a black background were stenciled. The piece was varnished first, and while the varnish was still sticky, gold powder was rubbed into it with a piece of velvet. Beautiful shaded effects may be obtained in this way. Designs also may be painted in gold with a brush. The gold paint comes in powder form with a bottle of banana oil. A little at a time is mixed with the oil according to directions, as this medium dries very fast. Silver and bronze also may be mixed with banana oil for painting.

Masking tape. Good effects can be obtained by accenting certain parts of a piece of furniture with straight lines of contrasting color. This often is done in chrome yellow on pieces painted black and stenciled in gold. If your hand is not steady enough to paint these lines with a fine brush, it is possible to buy masking tape at most paint stores which will help you to keep the lines straight and even. Place the gummed tape on both sides of where the line is to be painted, then paint the line, letting the paint run over the tape if it will. When the paint is almost dry, peel off the tape. This tape also is useful if you want to paint a wall in wide stripes or at any point where a straight sharp edge is essential.

Brush cleaner. Always rinse brushes in clear turpentine to dissolve the paint, then wash them with hot water and strong soap before putting them away. Smooth the hair of decorating brushes to a fine point while they are wet and let them dry that way. If a sable brush dries in a bent position, it may never work well again. If bristle brushes dry with paint on them, they may be softened with a good commercial brush cleaner, and they will be almost as good as new. Such a cleaner will also soften sable brushes, but they will never be quite the same again.

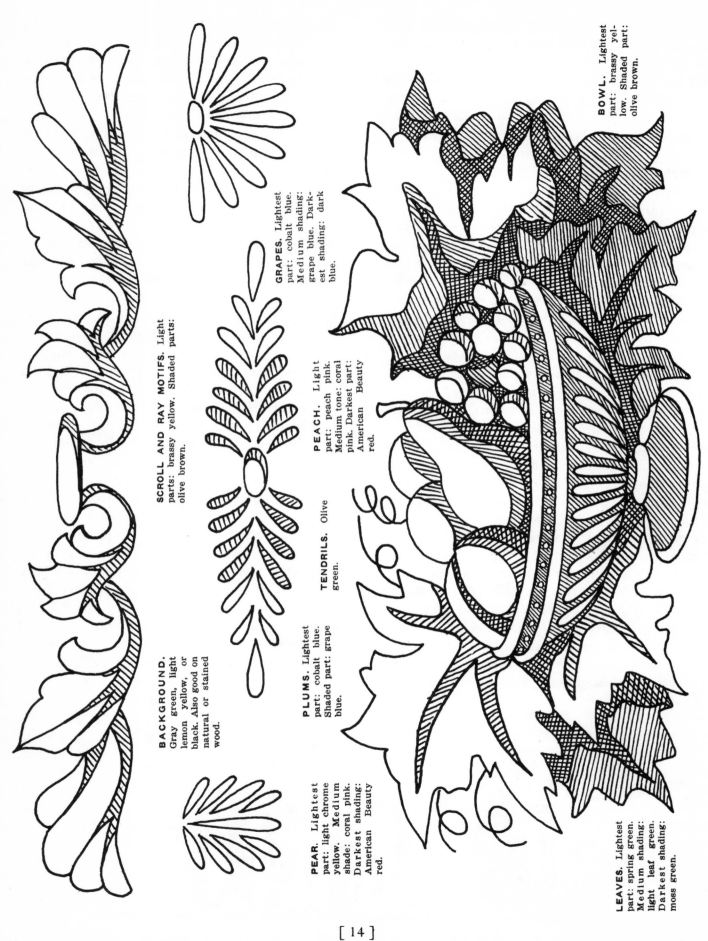

BOWL. Lightest part: brassy yellow. Shaded part: olive brown.

GRAPES. Lightest part: cobalt blue. Medium shading: grape blue. Darkest shading: dark blue.

PEACH. Light part: peach pink. Medium tone: coral pink. Darkest part: American Beauty red.

TENDRILS. Olive green.

SCROLL AND RAY MOTIFS. Light parts: brassy yellow. Shaded parts: olive brown.

PLUMS. Lightest part: cobalt blue. Shaded part: grape blue.

BACKGROUND. Gray green, light lemon yellow, or black. Also good on natural or stained wood.

PEAR. Lightest part: light chrome yellow. Medium shade: coral pink. Darkest shading: American Beauty red.

LEAVES. Lightest part: spring green. Medium shading: light leaf green. Darkest shading: moss green.

[14]

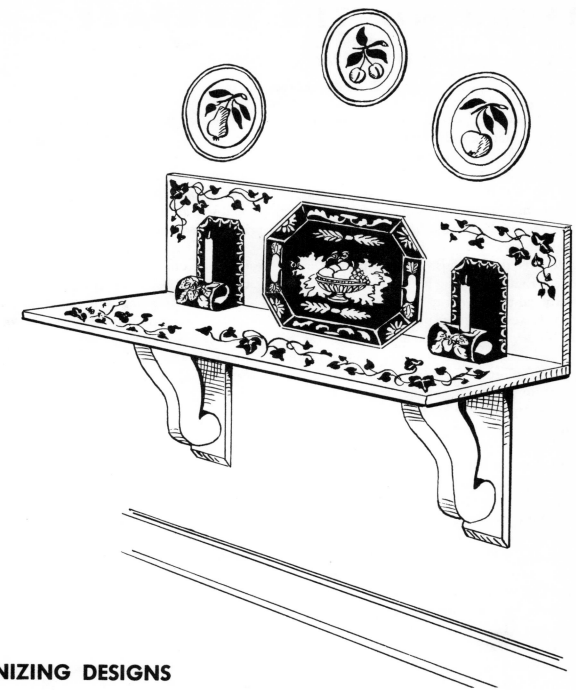

HARMONIZING DESIGNS

Good companions must be carefully chosen. That is as true of painting designs as of friends. An unusually happy combination of designs in shown here. The console is painted white, decorated in trailing sprays of ivy, and then heavily antiqued. This makes a perfect setting for the small articles all decorated in fruit designs. The three pieces with black backgrounds are used on the console shelf and add weight and importance to it. If dark pieces had been used above, the arrangement would have seemed top-heavy.

Those candle holders are really nothing but bent pieces of tin enameled black and decorated with little borders and bunches of strawberries. Holes were cut in the curled-over part of the tin, and the candles inserted through them. The plates on the wall are pie tins painted ivory white and decorated with fruit and colored bands. The tray is an old one appropriately decorated in a lovely old fruit and grape-leaf design. The painting patterns used for the articles shown may be found on pages 14, 44, 62, 69, and 127.

PREPARING THE SURFACE

A good background is essential for painted decorations

ALL the painting patterns in this book suggest suitable colors for the background of the design. Ivory, cream, gray greens, soft blues, and black are favorites. The ivory, cream, and black generally are used just as they come out of the can. It may be necessary to mix other colors as outlined under Color Formulas for painting patterns. But before we go into detail about colors let's be sure the surface of the article to be decorated is ready for paint. Do not be alarmed. Endless rubbing for old pieces that never were really valuable is not to be recommended. It is important, however, that the paint sticks and does not peel or blister. Here are some suggestions as to methods and materials that will give the best results with the least effort.

Why paint peels. One of the most usual reasons for paint peeling is that it has been used for a surface to which wax or furniture polish has been previously applied. Any kind of grease will cause paint to peel, even soap that has not been rinsed off. Sal soda is more efficient than soap in removing old grease or wax. A damp surface also can cause paint to peel. If water is used in cleaning, be sure the article is absolutely dry before applying paint. The safest method is to clean the surface with a rag moistened with turpentine. Several applications may be needed.

Preparing bare wood. Sand the wood, rubbing with the grain first, with medium-fine (No. 00) and then with fine (No. 000) sandpaper placed over a block of wood so that it may be gripped firmly. Wipe off the dust with a rag moistened with turpentine and then apply a priming coat of flat paint or undercoater.

Old finish in good condition. If old paint or varnish is in good condition and not scaling or cracked, generally it is not necessary to remove it. If the old varnish has a high gloss, it should be rubbed lightly with No. 000 sandpaper to dull the gloss and provide adhesion, as new paint is likely to peel off a glasslike surface. One coat of enamel without an undercoat of flat paint is usually enough over an old finish, but if the original finish is either much darker or much lighter than the new enamel, two coats may be required. The second coat of enamel may be

thinned slightly with turpentine so that it will flow on quickly and smoothly. The above treatment has proved to be satisfactory except for golden oak pieces finished with a heavy high-gloss varnish. If this varnish is not entirely removed, paint or enamel applied on it will almost always blister in time, though it may last quite a long while.

Old finish in bad condition. An old finish that is scaling off, that shows cracks or is blistered, must be removed before applying a new finish. Old paint that is still adhering well to the surface but was not applied smoothly may be rubbed down with No. 00 and then No. 000 sandpaper before applying a new finish. If the old finish must be removed, a good commercial paint and varnish remover is far quicker than the old sal soda and lye method. After the paint or varnish has been removed and all traces of acid and grease have been cleaned off, an undercoat of flat paint will be needed as for new bare wood.

Remove hardware. It is always best to remove metal and even wooden drawer pulls, handles, and knobs before painting or removing an old finish. Hinges and key plates should be removed too if possible. This not only prevents hardware from being marred, but it insures a smooth even surface for the entire piece.

Using paint and varnish remover. Always buy the best quality of paint and varnish remover and carefully read the directions that come with it. Generally the best results are obtained if the remover is brushed on sparingly one coat right after another until the surface is past the sticky stage and has become crumbly; then it is time to begin to scrape with the grain of wood, using a three-inch or four-inch paint scraper. A small portion of the piece may be done at one time, and the surface may be moistened a little with more remover if it gets too dry. Remember that the acid in the remover is very strong. Buy a cheap brush to apply the remover, as the acid will eat into your good brushes. This being so, it is not difficult to imagine what the acid would do to gloveless hands or anything on which it might drip or splatter. Protect everything with a thick layer of papers. Burn all rags used immediately. Scrub and then rinse away all traces of acid and grease, and allow the piece to dry thoroughly before applying an undercoat of flat paint as a base for enamel.

Fill holes and cracks. Plastic wood is better than putty for filling cracks and nail and screw holes. Apply it with a putty knife or any knife with a short wide blade. When it is dry, it may be sanded smooth.

Watch out for dust. Professionals who do fine refinishing make a point of sprinkling the floor of the workroom to lay the dust before applying paint or varnish. Also, before applying a new finish, they never fail to go over the surface with a clean rag moistened with turpentine to remove any last traces of dust. The amateur often fails to wipe off the dust after sandpapering the surface. He or she is likely to paint out of doors on a windy day. The result is a rough finish with dust sticking permanently in the paint or varnish. It may not be practical always to sprinkle the floor, but it is possible to avoid sweeping just before painting and to take other simple precautions.

Brushwork. Flat paint, enamel, and varnish require very little brushing. Spread a brushful on about a square foot at a time and smooth it off quickly with as few strokes as possible to be sure that it does not pile up or hang at any point. Once this is done, this finished area should not be touched with the brush again. A good bristle brush is necessary if you wish to obtain a perfectly smooth surface. For painting furniture a one-and-a-half-inch or two-inch flat brush is best. A one-inch flat brush is useful for small objects.

The first coat of paint. Either a prepared undercoater or a good flat paint should be used for a base coat on bare wood. White undercoater or flat paint may be tinted with pure color in oil or any good oil paint or enamel to produce special colors. When this base coat is dry and hard, sand it with No. 000 sandpaper and then wipe with a cloth moistened with turpentine before applying enamel.

Drying time. Undercoaters and flat paints usually dry sufficiently for a second coat in twenty-four hours. Some enamel dries quicker than others. At least twenty-four hours should be allowed before applying a second coat or beginning to decorate. If at the end of that time the surface is still the least bit sticky, do not apply any more paint until the surface is hard. New paint applied over sticky enamel dissolves the first coat, which then never becomes hard.

A mat finish. The traditional way to build up a hard but slightly dull finish for the background of painted designs was to paint the object to be decorated with a number of coats of gloss enamel, each rubbed with fine sandpaper or steel wool after it was thoroughly dry and hard. Today, modern enamels flow on so smoothly that most of this rubbing may be eliminated. A mat finish is usually obtained by using either a prepared semigloss enamel or by adding flat paint or undercoater to a high-gloss enamel. A half-and-half mixture produces about the right sheen. The more flat paint that is added to the enamel, the duller the sheen will be. A fourth way that a mat finish is produced is by mixing clear spar varnish with flat paint for the final coat. The proportion is usually about four parts flat paint and one part varnish. Any of these mixtures may be tinted with pure color in oil to produce special colors. One coat of semigloss paint or enamel is usually enough over a base coat of flat paint or an old finish. If another coat is required to cover, it may be thinned very slightly with turpentine to insure a smooth and flawless surface. When this is dry, you are ready to transfer the decorating design.

Preparing metals for painting. If you want paint to adhere to an article of tin or any other metal, the first step is to wash the piece with turpentine or with very hot water and sal soda to remove all trace of grease. The next step is to smooth any rough spots with No. 000 sandpaper or fine steel wool; then carefully wipe off all dust. In painting trays and other articles of tin, some artists always use a base or priming coat of red lead or other rust-inhibitive paint. This is essential if the object has started to rust, and when the red lead coat has been sanded smooth with fine steel wool, it makes a good base for one or more coats of either high-gloss or semigloss enamel. Varnish of the best quality also is used sometimes as a base coat on metals and is especially good if there are irregularities in the surface which it will fill in to some extent. Sand the varnish lightly and dust the surface before applying enamel. Automobile enamel or other metal enamel may be applied directly on the metal after it has been cleaned, or the piece may be sprayed with metal enamel.

Marbled effects. Chests, tables, and desks with panels or tops painted to resemble marble are extremely smart, and since marble comes in a great variety of colorings, they may be made to harmonize

Painted articles are used here to add design and color interest to a corner of a living room. A large box is decorated with a red heart, and a smaller box repeats the red with a quaint strawberry design. A bird is painted in soft colors on a round wooden plaque, and a tin plant container is painted green decorated in gold. A lamp and step table are painted antique ivory with green ivy, and a cigarette box on the stand is also hand decorated. All these things are full of charm. Yet anyone can make them for next to nothing, and paint them by tracing designs and filling in the colors. The patterns used may be found on pages 33, 41, 44, 62, 86, and 127.

with almost any decorations. It is also fun to paint a wooden bench out of doors to resemble marble, and it is practical to marbleize an old linoleum. Good color combinations are black veined with buff and yellow, blue veined with gray and white, white veined with gray and green and a touch of black. Use two coats of enamel for the background color. The veining is applied while the top coat is still wet. Your largest pointed brush and a pointed feather will be needed and your regular flat background brush for blending. Put in the heaviest veins first with the pointed brush, then blend them with the flat brush wiped very dry. Now put in veins of another color running in the opposite direction to the first ones, using the tip of the feather this time. Blend these slightly with the dry flat brush where they cross the first veins. When dry, varnish with two heavy coats of spar varnish.

TRANSFERRING DESIGNS

The materials and methods used for tracing outlines

DESIGNS generally are transferred by tracing the outlines of the pattern onto the article with transfer paper after the background is thoroughly dry. In most cases this is done with ordinary carbon paper such as every stenographer uses, which may be purchased in any stationery store. White and yellow transfer paper similar to carbon paper is useful for transferring designs onto dark backgrounds. Usually this may be purchased at an artists' supply store. If you cannot buy it, a substitute may be made by chalking paper with white or yellow wax crayon. Other materials that are essential are a soft pencil, and a hard one, pen and ink, and tough white transparent tracing paper such as architects use. The latter may be obtained at artists' supply stores. It is needed for making duplicate patterns traced from the ones in the book. Scotch tape also will be useful for anchoring tracing papers.

In making tracings, both for the duplicate pattern and in transferring the design, take plenty of time and follow the outlines accurately. If you pay attention to detail in making the tracings, when you start to paint you will find that the clear outline is not only a great aid but that it has given you a better understanding of the design. Do not think of the tracing as being a purely mechanical process. Try to get the feel of the design as you trace. Notice how the lines turn to make an interesting composition and try to sense the swing of each curve as you follow its outline. This will prepare you to paint the design without losing any of its style. A design that you trace or copy will never be dull and lifeless if you enter into its spirit in this way.

Duplicate patterns. There are several reasons for making a duplicate of the pattern in the book. First, it may be handled freely in experimenting with placing the design for the best effect on the object to be decorated. Another reason is that the outlines show through the transparent paper of the duplicate so that they may be traced from either side. This makes it possible to reverse the design to face the way that is most suitable for the space to be filled.

Repeat designs also may be transferred to face each other by turning the transparent pattern. To make the duplicate pattern, place the tracing paper over the design you wish to trace, and tip it in place with Scotch tape which will peel off later without marring the book. Now is when you will need pen and ink for, if you use it instead of pencil for making the tracing, the duplicate will not only be sharper and more accurate but it will have a more permanent value. The lines will not smudge, and it may be used over and over. The pattern in the book may be used for your color guide or, if you wish to work out a different color scheme, it may be noted on the duplicate pattern.

Transferring designs to a light ground. Place carbon paper, with the carbon side down, over the point to be decorated, place the duplicate pattern over it and secure both pieces with Scotch tape; then trace over the outlines with a sharp pencil, being careful to go over all the lines. Remove the sheets and you are ready to paint. If you do not have carbon paper or if the carbon does not transfer well on a glossy surface, turn the pattern over and go over the outlines on the back with a soft lead pencil; then place the pattern, with the pencil side down, over the point to be decorated and trace or rub it from the back with some smooth, hard object. The pressure transfers the soft pencil lines. It is a good plan to leave one corner free so that you can peek at the work now and then to see whether you are making a clear outline.

Transferring designs to a dark ground. If the design is to be transferred to a black or other dark ground on which carbon or pencil lines will not show, use white or yellow transfer paper in the same manner that carbon paper is used. If this light transfer paper is not available, yellow or white wax crayon or chalk may be applied thickly to a sheet of ordinary paper as a substitute. Experiment with this on the particular surface with which you are working. Chalk is not very satisfactory as it rubs off easily. The wax crayon will not make a clear impression on some glossy enamels.

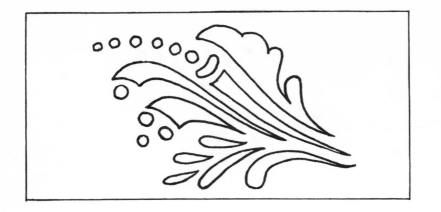

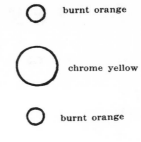

burnt orange

chrome yellow

burnt orange

BACKGROUND. Cream, powder blue, gray green, or black.

ROUND BUDS. Same as indicated in lower sketch.

LARGE FLOWERS. Chrome yellow, with tips of petals and center dot burnt orange.

LEAVES AND STEMS. All bottle green.

BORDER. Scallops: burnt orange. Dots: chrome yellow.

DESIGNS WITH MANY USES

Straight from Sweden come the three graceful motifs on the opposite page. The applications illustrate the manner in which designs may be used to give different effects. The tray has a black background, and the large motif repeated at each side of the three dots makes a wholly different design than when used singly in a smaller space. Even the little border seems to have a different character than when related more closely to the central motif.

The two boxes are especially attractive. One has a blue background, and gray green is used for the other. Both are finished with several coats of clear varnish and no antiquing. The shallow tin box is the kind in which fifty cigarettes used to be packaged. It is perfect for assorted buttons, as they can be spread out while you look for the desired size. The other box is a tin candy box which is very decorative in an open space on a bookshelf. It is used by a scrapbook fan to hold equipment for cutting and pasting clippings.

The wooden letter holder is something that any boy with a jig saw or a hand coping saw could make. The one shown here has a cream-colored background and has been given an antique finish after painting. The lamp, as you have probably guessed, is one of the glass coffee jars that we all know so well. If you could see it in color, you would not guess its origin so quickly. The whole jar, top and all, was painted gray green before the design was applied.

WALL DESIGNED TO FIT

Beyond a doubt the wall treatment is the most exciting feature of this bedroom, but there are so many interesting side lights that we better begin at the beginning. The fact is that most of the budget for bedroom furniture was spent for the best box springs and mattresses that could be found. And then the fun began with very little but imagination and a will to make the rest of the room live up to those comfortable beds.

The first step was bases for the box springs. These were made in the simplest possible manner of pieces of two-by-four pine, then headpieces cut out of three-quarter-inch plywood were screwed to the bases. A bedside stand also was made of the plywood by just screwing pieces together with angle irons to make top, sides, and shelves. The angle irons were placed well back so that they would not show from the front. All edges of the heads of the beds and the stand were then sanded thoroughly, and the pieces were given a priming coat of Firzite, which is an especially prepared resin and oil product that helps to keep the grain of plywood from show-

ing through paint or enamel. Two coats of mat-finish cream-colored enamel followed this.

A pink rose was painted in one corner of each bed head, and birds in opposite corners, both traced from patterns given here. Strands of ribbon in two tones of blue were then added. You will notice that the twist of the ribbon is not exactly the same for the two beds. Lines with the proper flourish were worked out on wrapping paper and then traced. The lamp base was made from a tin canister. The top and bottom were painted blue and the sides cream color. Roses were then fitted together to form a solid border around the can. One rose was painted on a cream-colored shade finished with blue at the edges.

There was an enormous stretch of blank cream-colored wall over the beds and nothing but a pair of fashion prints to fill it. Something daring and really dramatic was needed to give those beds a proper setting. The answer was this stunning bunch of roses painted in the center over the lamp with a bird at each side, with rosebuds and blue ribbon painted to appear as though the prints are hung from it.

DRESSING TABLE MAGIC

It is an old trick and yet it always seems like magic when a kitchen table or a box is made to look like Cinderella ready for the ball. A number of new twists are given to the trick here. Since the spreads for the beds, shown on the opposite page, were tufted on a foundation of unbleached muslin, it was decided to use this inexpensive material for the skirts of dressing table and stool. A small kitchen table with a drawer was found, but it had been standing out in the weather for so long that the top was too warped to use. It was replaced with a plywood top, cut to fit the table base without projecting much beyond the sides and front of the frame. A wood box from the grocery store was also fitted with a smooth piece of wood to make the top of the stool.

A mirror with a plain wood frame cost very little, and it must be admitted that it did not look very luxurious. These three bits of next to nothing were not a very promising start. Even when the mirror was hung with a blue ribbon and a rose-colored glass curtain tieback knob the combination lacked glamour. It was not until Cinderella put roses in her hair that the situation took a turn for the better. The top of the table and the stool, also the mirror frame, were enameled blue to contrast with the cream-colored skirt and wall. A big pink rose and a bud were then painted at opposite corners of the table and stool tops. The ruffles around these painted tops were made very full and pert. The one for the table could be turned back to permit the drawer to be opened.

Still the mirror seemed inadequate. Again the roses were used. This time the transparent tracing of the design was turned, as described in the instructions for transferring, so that the sprays of roses faced in opposite directions to frame the mirror and give it a great air of distinction. The final touch is the old imitation ivory comb, brush, and mirror set, and the pair of bottles all decked out in pink rosebuds. The stoppers of the bottles are wooden knobs such as may be purchased for drawer pulls. These are screwed into the tops of corks and then enameled blue to match the other blues in the room.

Another way that large roses may be used is to paint them on fabric for a dressing table skirt, draperies or a bedspread. The method and materials to use are fully described on page 13. In this way un-

bleached muslin, the best parts of an old sheet or any inexpensive cotton material may be turned into a handsome flowered fabric with very little effort. If you want to do something really exquisite and of lasting value, paint the design on sheer organdie or crisp taffeta. Roses painted in the simple manner that this pattern indicates are especially suitable for fabric painting. They may be arranged in an all-over design or sprays and single flowers may be placed to give accent wherever needed.

ROSE COLORS. If roses are to be painted pink, paint the lightest part pink, the medium shading American Beauty rose, and the darkest shading American Beauty red. For red roses, use vermilion, dark red, and wine red.

STEMS. Main stems: medium and dark brown. Small stems: light leaf green.

BACKGROUND. Ivory, cream, any neutral tone, or black.

LEAVES. Lightest part: spring green. Medium shading: light leaf green. Dark shading: bottle green.

HALLS ARE FUN TO PAINT

Like a stepchild—that is the way halls are treated in the average home. They are either ignored or else dressed up in castoffs from other parts of the house. If the hall is big enough to hold a piece of furniture, a table or a chair that is no longer useful anywhere else is placed there. All the unimportant, uninteresting pictures are hung in the hall, including photographs of relatives. Perhaps that is to be expected. At best, most halls are not very attractive. Their proportions are often bad, and if they are in the inner regions of the house, they are likely to be dark and dreary.

Yes, it is true that no one spends much time in any hall. Perhaps it is wasteful to place choice things there that are needed elsewhere. It seems rather silly to furnish a hall as though someone were going to settle down and live there. That is just the point. No one ever settles down in a hall, but they do get an impression as they pass through. And how many thousands of times one does pass through most halls! Why shouldn't this passing acquaintance include a bright hello or a cheerful greeting? Not a trite "Is it hot enough for you?" or "It looks like rain."

If you pay a little attention to any hall, it will perk right up and develop quite a personality of its own. The tiny hall sketched here seemed about as hopeless as any that you could imagine. It was narrow and dark with doors on all sides. Any rug placed on the floor was sure to be a hazard either because it was always being kicked up or because it interfered with opening doors. When the walls, woodwork, and doors were painted white, it gave the effect of half a dozen lights turned on, but the place was still as uninteresting as an empty icebox. It was at this point that the lady of the house took over with some painting ideas of her own.

Both of the large roses in the pattern on the opposite page were used on the door panels—the larger one at the upper right of each panel, and the smaller one in the opposite corner. A striking effect was needed here, so the roses were painted in the red coloring suggested on the pattern instead of in the pink tones. These stunning big red roses and green leaves on a pure white ground were indeed a cheering sight.

What could be more logical than to paint a rug on the floor? The wax was scrubbed off with turpentine so that the paint would be sure to stick. Scrolls from the pattern on page 26 were then transferred to form a border, and were painted in the brassy yellows suggested on the pattern. In the center, the rose pattern was used once again, with the largest rose in the middle and the smaller one with the bud repeated at each side. When the paint was dry, three coats of the best quality of clear varnish were applied to protect the design. Wax was then applied, and the floor thereafter treated in the same manner as in other parts of the house.

USING LARGE SCROLLS. These motifs may be used as borders or fillers wherever a bold effect is wanted, as for the painted rug on page 25 or the large wardrobe on page 54. They may be developed in any of the colorings suggested here to harmonize with other motifs.

BACKGROUND. Scrolls show to good advantage on any background that is several tones lighter than the lightest color used. Also good on very dark contrasting colors and on black.

GREEN COLORING. Lightest part: light leaf green. Medium shade: dark leaf green. Darkest part: bottle green.

BRASSY COLORING. Lightest part: light lemon yellow. Medium tone: brassy yellow. Darkest part: olive brown.

GOLD COLORING. Lightest part: chrome yellow. Medium tone: orange. Darkest part: medium brown.

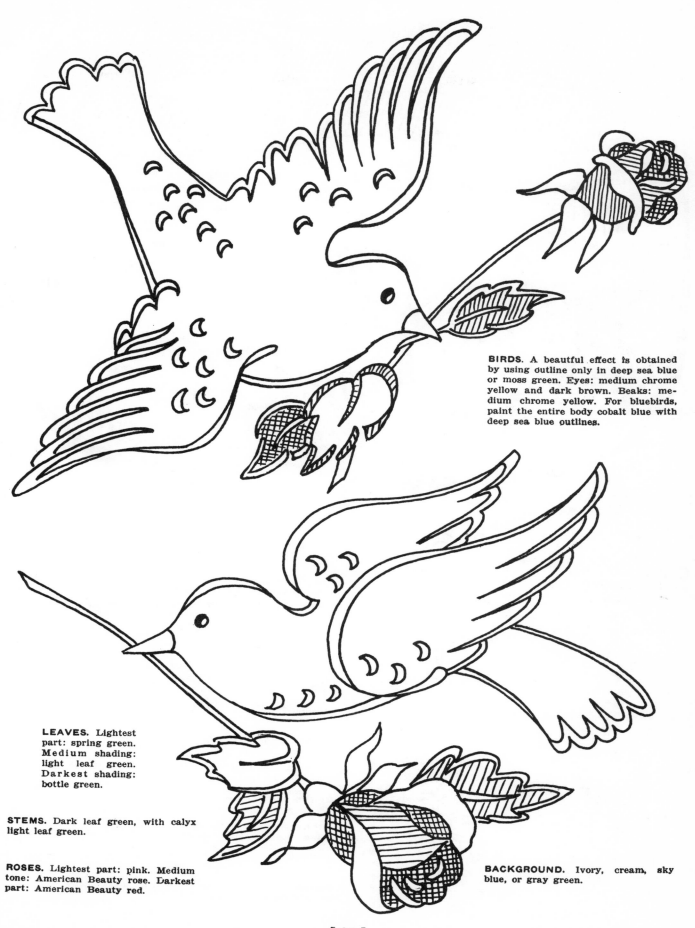

BIRDS. A beautful effect is obtained by using outline only in deep sea blue or moss green. Eyes: medium chrome yellow and dark brown. Beaks: medium chrome yellow. For bluebirds, paint the entire body cobalt blue with deep sea blue outlines.

LEAVES. Lightest part: spring green. Medium shading: light leaf green. Darkest shading: bottle green.

STEMS. Dark leaf green, with calyx light leaf green.

ROSES. Lightest part: pink. Medium tone: American Beauty rose. Darkest part: American Beauty red.

BACKGROUND. Ivory, cream, sky blue, or gray green.

SNOW CRYSTALS. White on any of the blue backgrounds suggested here.

BACKGROUND. The snow scene framed in ribbon and the snow crystals may be painted on either a medium dark or a light blue ground.

SKY. Follow the sky blue formula for color, but let it be a little darker toward the horizon. Blend into clouds with a dry brush.

SNOW AND CLOUDS. Trace the ribbon frame first and then paint the whole space inside the frame white. Allow to dry and then transfer the rest of the design onto the white surface. The snow and clouds are left white as the rest of the design is painted. Shadows outlining hills and on house and barn roof: sky blue.

ROAD AND PATH. Taupe gray is used for the ruts in the road, shading into dark brown toward the barn door and for the path to the house.

HOUSE. Front: white. Shaded part: lines in sky blue. Dark brown shadow under eaves and along base of front.

MAILBOX. Post and front of box: dark brown. Side of box: American vermilion.

HEDGES. Fine lines in dark brown or a continuous dark brown shadow under the snow-topped hedges.

BARNS AND CHIMNEY. Dark side: American vermilion. Light side: coral. Doors, windows, and inside of chimney: dark brown.

TREES. All dark brown or a combination of dark and medium brown with the dark side toward the left of the picture.

SHRUBS. Those around the house: dark brown. Shrubs in distance and at lower right: medium brown.

RIBBON. Darkest part: wine red. Medium shade: dark red. Lightest part: American vermilion.

PIQUANT AS A WINTER DAY

A Victorian bowknot tied around a snow scene and the fascinating shapes of crystals against a clear blue background are enough to start a search for the old sleigh bells and lap robe. The whole idea has a romantic flavor which is in keeping with things that are old and amusing for things that are new. The scene is easy to paint if you are fairly good at fine brushwork. The trick is in keeping the contrasts sharp and clean.

This is the type of scene that used to be painted at the tops of mirrors, though the mailbox on the post was a thing unknown in the good old days. Even an inexpensive modern mirror decorated in this way will take on quite an air. A fairly long mirror is needed, as about seven inches at the top will be devoted to the decoration.

When painting the upper part of a mirror, it will be helpful to use masking tape across the glass. When the tape is removed a good straight edge results. The frame of the mirror shown here matches the blue background for the snow crystals. If a contrasting frame is used, you will have to be careful about not smudging it, but it is not advisable to remove the mirror from the frame while working, as there is so much possibility of marring the back. As always when painting on glass, avoid using oil for thinning the paint. A little varnish and a dash of japan drier makes the best thinner for this work.

The snow crystals painted in white on a blue ground are decorative for small objects. They make good borders in formal rows, as used on the flat box shown here. For a good scattered informal arrangement, as shown on the wastebasket and jar top, toss small coins on the surface and then mark the spots where they fall.

You have probably thought of using these designs for Christmas cards. If you write Christmas notes, one or two crystals in white tempera color on a blue paper will be refreshing and individual. Large cards worthy of being framed are more and more the mode, but if you want to paint smaller ones the left side of this snow scene may be used in a smaller frame of ribbon.

A PAINTED WINDOW SHADE

Design interest does not have to be reserved for the draperies at the sides of windows. Beautiful effects may be obtained by painting a striking motif in oil paint on an ordinary window shade. Here, extra vine sprays are given to add to the bird design on the opposite page.

VINE WITH BERRIES. Stems: dark brown. Leaves: dark leaf green. Berries: rusty red, with dark brown tips.

CREST. Bottle green, with cobalt blue tips.

EYE. Medium brown, with lemon yellow edge.

Spot on breast and wing: wine red.

bottle green

cobalt blue

BEAK. Lemon yellow.

Bottle green, with large dots wine red, and small dots cobalt blue.

Cobalt blue, with wine red dots.

bottle green

LEGS. Top: bottle green. Lower legs and feet: dark brown.

EXTRA S... sign ma... to fill a l... ing a... sp...

MATCHING BORDER. May be used separately or around edge of a tray, with bird design in center.

BACKGROUND. Gray green, light lemon yellow, or black. Also good on natural or stained wood.

DESIGN AND COLOR HARMONY

Stray bits of advice are pretty well summed up here. It is when painted designs are the star attraction that you begin to lift humdrum furnishings out of drabness. Generally the best results are obtained by using designs that are in harmony with the feeling or spirit of the room—gay simple motifs for informal rooms, quaint designs for a room with a period feeling. Let one gayly decorated piece dominate the scene. Other less important pieces may then pick up the motif and repeat it throughout the room.

All of this has been said before, and here you see how it works out. A cheap drop-leaf table and chairs and a woven rag rug had a period feeling, but were not authentic reproductions of antiques. The table was elaborately decorated with a quaint heart and flower design and foliage sprays. The patterns for these are given on the opposite page and on page 61. Since this piece was not big enough to dominate the scene, its importance was built up or emphasized by the arrangement of three mirrors from the dime store and shadow boxes made out of a pair of discarded chest drawers.

Parts of the painting design used for the table were repeated on the glass of the mirrors, on scalloped facings for the tops of the shadow boxes, on painted bread pans used for flowers, on a workbox on the table, and on the side chairs. The seats of the chairs were painted red to match the large heart on the table leaf, and this repetition of strong color below eye level seemed to give weight at the base of the whole arrangement.

FLOWERS. Buds: cobalt blue with dark blue shadow. Large flowers near bottom: vermilion with dark red shadows. Two bell-shaped flowers: shaded part, dark blue with medium chrome yellow edging; dots and main part of flower, cobalt blue. Tulip-shaped flower at left: base petals, cobalt blue; center, vermilion; crossed petals, medium chrome yellow. Flower at center top: outside petals, medium chrome yellow; inside petals, vermilion. Top flower at right: center, vermilion, then medium chrome yellow and cobalt blue outside; stamens at tip, medium chrome yellow.

BACKGROUND. White, ivory, cream, olive, gray green, or black.

FOLIAGE. Stems and shaded leaves: bottle green. Light leaves: light leaf green.

HEART. Vermilion with shaded part dark red.

This sketch shows how a traced outline of a design may be used as a guide for painting brush-stroke flower petals, leaves, and other designs. Hold the brush in an almost perpendicular position, as shown, and steady your hand with the little finger resting on the work. The stroke is widened or tapered according to the pressure on the brush. Designs quite different in type and character may be made by combining brush strokes made in this manner.

BRUSH-STROKE DESIGNS

It is possible to get a great variety of effects by handling your brush freely and easily. The motifs shown on these two pages are wholly different in character, and yet most of the leaves, scrolls, and flower petals are formed by a single stroke of the brush. Small hearts require two strokes made like commas facing in opposite directions.

Skilled artists paint such designs freehand as quickly as a word is written. A beginner needs an outline to show where and how the strokes are to be made. The trick is in using a good brush that tapers to a fine point, holding it correctly, and learning to regulate the pressure to narrow or widen the stroke as required.

The brush should be held almost perpendicular as in the sketch on the opposite page. The pressure is regulated by the little finger which rests on the work and moves along as the stroke is made. Whenever possible, start the stroke at the wide end and taper it by easing the pressure on the brush. A more graceful and smoother stroke is obtained in this way than by starting at the point and increasing the pressure.

DESIGNS FOR A DUTCH CHEST

When William Penn invited the persecuted peoples along the reaches of the Rhine to come to America way back in 1681, they brought with them, stored in their minds and hearts, many things other than the will of each to worship God according to his own desires. There were many skilled craftsmen among those early settlers in Pennsylvania, and their descendants still remain in what we now call the Pennsylvania Dutch country. Many of their early crafts also remain and are much prized by collectors.

Perhaps the most beautiful of all their painted furniture are the elaborately decorated dower chests. Certainly no other pieces are more useful in a modern home. They are perfect for blanket chests or for storing anything from firewood to magazines. One of these chests is just the thing for an accent piece in any room. Their construction is always of the simplest sort, so that any good amateur cabinetmaker can make the framework for one. The designs painted on them also are easy to copy.

A set of patterns for the Dutch chest shown are given here on the following pages. They are interesting to paint or stencil in perfectly flat colors, and you may enjoy them even more if you know a little about their original meaning. The tulip symbolizes Lily Time or the golden age of peace and plenty promised the early Dutch settlers if they would come to the New World. The tree of life rising from an urn, the blade, the flower, the seed, and the heart-of-man are all symbols used over and over. The dove of peace appears frequently. Fruit and flowers symbolize God's bounty. Hex signs were used for luck and to keep away evil.

HEX SIGNS. The design above is painted on a white ground. The solid parts in the pattern are to be painted black. Parts of the inner star shown in line shading: vermilion. Outside points of star shown in light dots: medium chrome yellow. Tulips shown in heavy dots: cobalt blue. Leaves shown in medium shading: bottle green. The hex design on the opposite page is painted in black and yellow on a white ground.

TULIP DESIGN. The tulip in the design on the opposite page is painted medium chrome yellow with shaded part cobalt blue. Flower just below: vermilion with shaded part cobalt blue and stamens medium chrome yellow. Light parts of leaves and stems: light leaf green. Shaded parts: bottle green. Urn: vermilion.

The main part of this chest is enameled black, but the parts of the top and the front where the hex designs and panels are to be painted are enameled white first. The white spaces for the designs are then covered with stiff paper while the rest of the chest is being painted black. The tulip designs are traced on the black background between the white panels.

SIMPLE COLOR CONTRASTS

We think of colorful Dutch designs, and yet the range of their coloring is generally limited to red, bright Dutch blue, clear yellow, and rich green. Sometimes there is a slight effect of shading resulting from pressure on the brush or from overlapping strokes. That is all. The charm of the color depends on simple contrasts.

The arrangement and repetition of contrasts almost make the hex design shown here whirl like a pinwheel. On the opposite page is a Dutch design adapted for use as a stencil. Here again a lively effect is obtained with simple contrasts. Dutch pottery often is painted in black or white on a red ground. The same idea may be used for other things.

Try the little red and white design shown here on a box, and add a few flourishes of your own. The bird may be adapted to many uses by adding more or fewer branches to his perch, according to the size and shape of the space to be filled.

STENCIL OR TRACING PATTERN.
This design will hold together in one piece if cut out for a stencil pattern, or it may be traced and painted in the usual way.

BACKGROUND. The design may be used on a white, cream, powder blue, or black background.

COLORS FOR DESIGN. American vermilion, medium chrome yellow, cobalt blue, light leaf green, and bottle green are the colors used, as shown on page 38.

BACKGROUND. Powder blue, cream, or black.

SWAGS. Bottle green. Dots: medium chrome yellow.

BIRD. Head: vermilion. Crest, wing, and tail: bottle green. Eye, legs, and feet: dark brown. Bill, neck, and breast: lemon yellow. Breast and neck feathers: bottle green.

LEAVES AND SCROLLS. Shaded parts: bottle green. Light parts: apple green.

BERRIES. Medium chrome yellow with bottle green stems.

HEARTS. Vermilion.

FLOWER IN HEART. Cobalt blue, with medium chrome yellow center.

LIGHT, SHADE, AND CONTRAST

Quite distinct from the brush-stroke type of design are these motifs painted in flat color with lights and shadows sharply defined. Designs painted in this manner have a striking decorative quality that carries well even at some distance. This is an important thing to keep in mind in painting anything that is to be used with telling effect in a room decorating scheme.

Learn to think in terms of clear simple masses of light and shade. If softer shading is wanted, first paint the light, medium, and dark variations of each color as shown here. Then, while the paint is still wet, blend them together with an almost dry brush. Add brilliant highlights and dark accents last.

Keep the direction of the light consistent throughout the design whether from the top, bottom, or one side or the other. Think which way the shadows would fall and where the light would strike with greatest brilliance, and your shading will never be muddled and confused.

A SCANDINAVIAN DESIGN

From Norway and Sweden come flower and foliage designs in an engaging combination of naturalistic and conventional forms. Leaves have a way of turning into scrolls that conform to the shape of the object that is being decorated. The outlines of zinnias and marigolds are simplified and yet recognizable in fresh true colors.

These designs may be adapted to modern uses with wonderful effect. The motif shown here is repeated four times on the back of a nondescript chair, giving it no end of style and an entirely new start in life. It is used also to redecorate an old magazine rack, and a plywood tray and stand is made at home in this group by a repetition of the same design and colors.

BACKGROUND. Ivory, cream, gray green, or black.

IVY DESIGNS. These four motifs may be combined, repeated, and adapted to fill spaces effectively or to make borders.

STEMS. Leaf stems: dark leaf green. Main stems: medium brown.

LEAVES. Light leaf green, with shaded part bottle green. The veins of the leaves are light leaf green and may be painted last, after the bottle green part is dry.

[44]

TABLE MATS AND CHAIRS

Of all the things that you may paint, table mats will probably rate highest in usefulness. In most homes today, breakfast through dinner, they make their appearance on the table in one form or another. Feast or snack, party or food family style, they change their mood with the occasion. The colorful type in bold designs—the kind that may be washed with one swipe of a damp cloth—are most popular and with good reason. So lend the spice of variety to meals with a number of different kinds and have a set or two tied up in ribbon. They make wonderful gifts.

There are a number of different materials in which mats may be painted. Pressed cork is good and so is ordinary oilcloth. Heavy cardboard finished with a number of coats of spar varnish on both sides with special attention to the edges will last a long time. And if you want to, you can paint mats of fabric, which may be washed and ironed a reasonable number of times without fading. Sprays of ivy on a white ground are used for the mats shown here, and a set of green and white chairs used with them are particularly inviting. There are any number of other designs in this book that would be equally attractive. Morning-glories or strawberries are especially recommended. Mexican designs are bold and gay for some kinds of parties. Animals and marching children will please the youngsters.

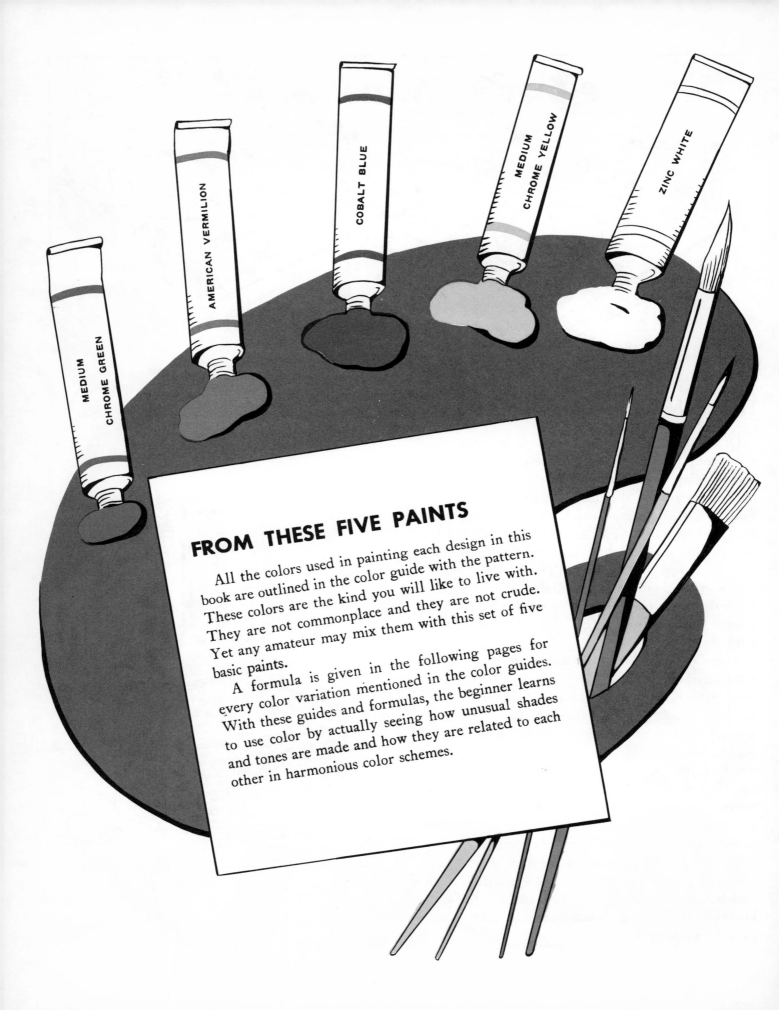

MEDIUM CHROME GREEN

AMERICAN VERMILION

COBALT BLUE

MEDIUM CHROME YELLOW

ZINC WHITE

FROM THESE FIVE PAINTS

All the colors used in painting each design in this book are outlined in the color guide with the pattern. These colors are the kind you will like to live with. They are not commonplace and they are not crude. Yet any amateur may mix them with this set of five basic paints.

A formula is given in the following pages for every color variation mentioned in the color guides. With these guides and formulas, the beginner learns to use color by actually seeing how unusual shades and tones are made and how they are related to each other in harmonious color schemes.

COLOR FORMULAS

*More than sixty shades and tones
from five tubes of paint*

OPEN the icebox door and you have before you the kinds of colors that delight an artist's soul. If there is a tomato there, it is not just red, it is a special red. There may be grapes that are a deep rich blue as distinctive as the flavor of the fruit itself. The yellow of a lemon is not at all the same as the yellow of butter. Olives are green like no other green. Place one on a lettuce leaf, add a sprig of parsley, and you have three distinct greens, each with a quality all its own. Anyone who loves color enough to want to paint enjoys these subtle color differences.

One of the things that I especially wanted to do in planning the colors for the patterns in this book was to give a carefully harmonized color scheme for each, using shades and tones with these subtle qualities—the kinds of colors that are a thrill to use. Yet I did not want to suggest the purchase of an elaborate set of expensive paints. Theoretically any color can be mixed by using combinations of pure red, yellow, and blue paint pigments. However, pigments have certain inherent qualities that cause them to react in different ways when combined. What then was the minimum number of paint colors that could be used successfully to mix this wide and well-balanced range of unusual shades and tones?

This question led to literally hundreds of experiments. In the end, five basic paint colors were selected. They are American vermilion, medium chrome yellow, cobalt blue, medium chrome green, and zinc white. These were the only colors used in working out the more than sixty color formulas given here. If clear black is needed for any part of a design, ivory black may be added to this list. No black paint is used in any of these color formulas, though there is a formula for mixing a black with a brownish cast. This brownish black is the nearest thing to pure black that it is possible to mix with the five basic paints. In most designs it gives a softer effect than would be obtained with dead black. Backgrounds are another matter. They are usually painted with a mat-finish enamel, and if black is indicated in the pattern it should be a good clear pure black.

The paints for this basic set of colors may be obtained in artists' tube oil colors as well as in water colors. The pure pigments ground in oil also come in tubes, but they should not be confused with artists' tube oil colors which are ready for use just as they are. Pure color in oil is much stronger than prepared paint and must be mixed with a base, such as white lead or zinc white, before they have the right spreading consistency for painting. Many ordinary paint stores now handle artists' tube oil colors, or they may be found in artists' supply stores.

When you are buying the five basic paints, keep in mind that American vermilion is quite different from English or Chinese vermilion. They both have an orange cast that makes a muddy color when used in any formula with blue in it. There are three chrome yellows: lemon chrome, medium chrome, and orange chrome. It is the medium chrome yellow that you want for these formulas. No other blue will give the same results as cobalt blue. Be sure to get the deepest cobalt. It is about the color of what is generally called royal blue, not light like Dutch blue. It is medium not light or dark chrome green that you need. Zinc white is used instead of lead white because lead has a chemical reaction on cobalt blue which causes it to darken. Ivory black is recommended instead of lampblack because it dries quicker and because some lampblacks are quite acid and are therefore not good to use for tin trays and other things made of metal.

So now you have five tubes of paint from which you could make hundreds, perhaps thousands of color variations. If you are a little aghast at the thought of using even sixty colors, remember that seldom more than five or six are required in any one design. Sometimes you will use fewer than that. In working out these formulas, the colors actually were matched up with the lemons and oranges and olives and tomatoes out of the icebox and with other everyday things that everyone knows. They have been given names that will help to identify them with familiar things. You are not on strange ground, though your eyes may be opened to things you have never seen.

In actually mixing these colors on your palette, you will not measure each part exactly, but the exact formula before you will help to gauge the amount of each basic pigment to take on your brush or palette knife. It is one thing to tell you that coral pink is vermilion with a dash of white and a trace of yellow. It is another to tell you how much to use of each. Even if you measure only with your eye, you are far more likely to blend a good lively coral color on the first try. By seeing the formula and the result at the same time, you soon gain a sense of color proportion. It will not be long before you begin to recognize the color make-up of unusual shades and tones. Then you really will be seeing color accurately as an artist sees it. If you are going to use much of any one color, mix it in a glass jar with a tight top. It is easier to measure accurately then. A set of measuring spoons as used in cooking is useful for this purpose. Take only a little of the color on your palette at a time and keep the jar tightly closed.

The basic pigments used for painting the patterns shown in this book are: American vermilion, medium chrome yellow, cobalt blue, medium chrome green, and zinc white.

Reds and pinks

Pinks are really light reds—that is, red with a large proportion of white added. Most reds and pinks lean slightly either toward blue or toward yellow. The amount of blue or yellow added to the basic red determines the cast or hue of the color. Reds and pinks are grayed or darkened to a rather muddy color by adding the complementary color of red which is green—a combination of blue and yellow. To avoid a muddy red, blue only is used to darken the reds suggested here.

Vermilion: American vermilion is the basic color for all the red and pink mixtures given here. It is the nearest to pure red of any paint. It may be given the orange cast of English and Chinese vermilion by adding 1 part chrome yellow to 4 parts American vermilion, but there is no way to give it quite the brilliance that these pigments have.

Tomato red: 10 parts American vermilion; 1 part medium chrome yellow.

Rusty red: 5 parts American vermilion; 1 part medium chrome yellow.

Lacquer red: 4 parts American vermilion; 1 part medium chrome yellow.

Terra-cotta red: 2 parts American vermilion; 1 part chrome yellow.

Flamingo red: 6 parts American vermilion; 1 part medium chrome yellow; 1 part zinc white.

Dark coral: 3 parts American vermilion; 1 part medium chrome yellow; 4 parts zinc white.

Light coral: 2 parts American vermilion; 3 parts medium chrome yellow; 30 parts zinc white.

Shell pink: 2 parts American vermilion; 3 parts medium chrome yellow; 50 parts zinc white.

Peach pink: 1 part American vermilion; 5 parts medium chrome yellow; 50 parts zinc white.

Flesh pink: 1 part American vermilion; 5 parts medium chrome yellow; 100 parts zinc white.

The variations listed above are of yellowish reds and pinks. The last five should really be classified with the orange group because they have more yellow than red in them. However, since we think of them as red and pink, it is interesting to consider them here and note how they differ from other reds and pinks. The following are reds and pinks with a blue cast.

Dark red: 10 parts American vermilion; 1 part cobalt blue.

Wine red: 3 parts American vermilion; 1 part cobalt blue.

Strawberry red: 20 parts American vermilion; 1 part cobalt blue; 1 part chrome yellow; 10 parts zinc white.

Ashes of roses: 15 parts American vermilion; 2 parts cobalt blue; 1 part chrome yellow; 30 parts zinc white.

American Beauty red: 1 part American vermilion; 1 part zinc white.

American Beauty rose: 3 parts American vermilion; 10 parts zinc white.

Pink (light rose): 1 part American vermilion; 10 parts zinc white.

Yellow, orange tones, and browns

The light tints of yellow are made by adding white. They do not show up well in a painting design unless they are used on a dark background. Greenish yellows are made by adding blue. When red is added to yellow, the color becomes orange. The complement of yellow is violet—a combination of red and blue. If this red and blue combination is added to yellow, brilliance of color is lost as is always the case when red, yellow, and blue are combined. Yellow grayed in this manner becomes a lifeless uninteresting color.

Chrome yellow: Medium chrome yellow is used in mixing all the yellow, orange, and brown formulas given here. It is the nearest to pure yellow of any paint pigment.

Light chrome yellow (butter color): 3 parts medium chrome yellow; 2 parts zinc white.

Cream: 1 part medium chrome yellow; 20 parts zinc white. This mixture has more life or brilliance than ready-mixed cream paint which is generally made with raw sienna or yellow ochre and white. A little chrome yellow may be added to these rather dull prepared mixtures to liven them.

Ivory: 1 part medium chrome yellow; 70 parts zinc white.

Above is a good list of clear yellows and yellow tints. The next three are the greenish yellows which are so often combined with olive green and olive brown in these designs.

Lemon yellow: 20 parts medium chrome yellow; 1 part cobalt blue.

Light lemon yellow: 20 parts medium chrome yellow; 1 part cobalt blue; 40 parts zinc white.

Brassy yellow: 10 parts medium yellow; 1 part cobalt blue.

Olive brown: 2 parts medium chrome yellow; 1 part American vermilion; 2 parts cobalt blue.

The following formulas are for orange and brown, and it is interesting to note how red, and then red and blue, added to yellow changes it through orange to brown, and then to almost pure black.

Carrot yellow: 5 parts medium chrome yellow; 1 part American vermilion.

Orange: 10 parts medium chrome yellow; 1 part American vermilion.

Burnt orange: 1 part medium chrome yellow; 1 part American vermilion.

Sun tan: 3 parts medium chrome yellow; 1 part American vermilion; 50 parts zinc white.

Tan: 2 parts medium chrome yellow; 1 part American vermilion; 1 part cobalt blue; 3 parts zinc white.

Golden tan: 5 parts medium chrome yellow; 1 part American vermilion; 1 part cobalt blue; 15 parts zinc white.

Medium brown: 1 part medium chrome yellow; 2 parts American vermilion; 2 parts cobalt blue.

Dark brown: 1 part medium chrome yellow; 5 parts American vermilion; 10 parts cobalt blue.

Brownish black: 2 parts medium chrome yellow; 1 part American vermilion; 8 parts cobalt blue.

A dozen different blues

Most blues lean slightly toward green or toward violet. Greenish blues are made by adding either yellow or green to blue. The violet blues given here are mixed by adding red to blue. The proportion of yellow, green, or red added determines the cast or hue of the blue. The complement of blue is orange —a red and yellow combination. Even a small amount of red and yellow added to blue turns it to brown or gray, as may be seen in the gray and brown formulas given here.

Cobalt blue: This is the basic color used for all the blues listed here. It is a clear rich bright blue and is nearer to pure blue than any other paint pigment with the same intense brilliance.

Medium cobalt (Dutch blue): 1 part cobalt blue; 1 part zinc white.

Powder blue: 1 part cobalt blue; 10 parts zinc white.

Flag blue: 10 parts cobalt blue; 1 part American vermilion.

Dark blue (navy blue): 5 parts cobalt blue; 2 parts American vermilion.

Grape blue: 2 parts cobalt blue; 1 part American vermilion.

Periwinkle blue: 2 parts cobalt blue; 1 part American vermilion; 5 parts zinc white.

The above are the pure blues and the blues with a violet cast. The following is a set of five good greenish blues.

Deep sea blue (quite a dark blue): 30 parts cobalt blue; 1 part medium chrome yellow.

Peacock blue: 3 parts cobalt blue; 1 part medium chrome green; 1 part zinc white.

China blue: 4 parts cobalt blue; 1 part medium chrome green; 4 parts zinc white.

Turquoise blue: 3 parts cobalt blue; 1 part medium chrome green; 10 parts zinc white.

Sky blue: 4 parts cobalt blue; 1 part medium chrome green; 20 parts zinc white.

Some useful greens

Green is a combination of yellow and blue. However, all blue pigments are extremely difficult to blend with yellow paints, and cobalt blue, which is the basic blue used for this series of formulas, does not have sufficient tinting strength to make strong clear greens. For these reasons, medium chrome green is used as the basic pigment for most of the greens listed here. The variations are obtained by adding yellow, blue, or white, or by graying the color by adding its complement which is red.

Chrome green: The medium chrome green used in mixing these colors is a vivid emerald green.

Apple green: 5 parts medium chrome green; 1 part medium chrome yellow; 2 parts zinc white.

Light apple green: 5 parts medium chrome green; 1 part medium chrome yellow; 10 parts zinc white.

Light leaf green: 2 parts medium chrome green; 1 part medium chrome yellow.

Dark leaf green: 15 parts medium chrome green; 1 part American vermilion.

Moss green: 15 parts medium chrome green; 4 parts American vermilion.

Cactus green: 15 parts medium chrome green; 4 parts American vermilion; 2 parts zinc white.

Bottle green (a very dark green): 4 parts cobalt blue; 2 parts medium chrome green; 1 part American vermilion.

Gray green: 2 parts cobalt blue; 1 part medium chrome yellow; 10 parts zinc white.

The above greens are all decidedly more green than yellow, though the bottle green is the only one that leans heavily toward blue. The following are three yellowish greens that are used in many beautiful color schemes.

Chartreuse: 4 parts medium chrome green; 5 parts medium chrome yellow; 1 part zinc white.

Spring green: 2 parts medium chrome green; 3 parts medium chrome yellow.

Olive green: 1 part cobalt blue; 1 part medium chrome yellow.

Six good grays

All these gray mixtures are made with red, yellow, blue, and white. The more blue there is in the formula, the colder the gray will be. As the amount of red and yellow increases in proportion to the amount of blue used the gray becomes warmer in tone. Most commercial grays are made with black and white, with umber or sienna added but they do not have as much warmth as the grays given here.

Silver gray: 10 parts cobalt blue; 3 parts American vermilion; 2 parts medium chrome yellow; 30 parts zinc white.

Gun-metal gray: 10 parts cobalt blue; 3 parts American vermilion; 2 parts medium chrome yellow; 15 parts zinc white.

Dove gray: 10 parts cobalt blue; 3 parts American vermilion; 3 parts medium chrome yellow; 15 parts zinc white.

Stone gray: 10 parts cobalt blue; 3 parts American vermilion; 3 parts medium chrome yellow; 50 parts zinc white.

Elephant gray: 7 parts cobalt blue; 3 parts American vermilion; 2 parts medium chrome yellow; 15 parts zinc white.

Taupe: 6 parts cobalt blue; 2 parts American vermilion; 1 part medium chrome yellow; 1 part zinc white.

Two violet-hued colors

All violet and purple colors are a combination of red and blue. Lavender tints are made by adding white. Cobalt blue is not strong enough to be used in making a brilliant royal purple, and any purple mixture made with it becomes quite gray when lightened with white. If brilliant purples and lavenders are wanted, use Prussian blue instead of cobalt, and Venetian red instead of American vermilion. The complement of violet is yellow, and the slightest trace of it in a purple mixture will gray the color. That is why blue red like Venetian is better to use than one that has even a slight hint of yellow in it. However, the two violet colors given here, made with American vermilion and cobalt, are not muddy, though they do not have brilliance. No other purples are needed for the patterns in this book.

Plum color: 2 parts American vermilion; 1 part cobalt blue.

Heliotrope: 2 parts American vermilion; 1 part cobalt blue; 4 parts zinc white.

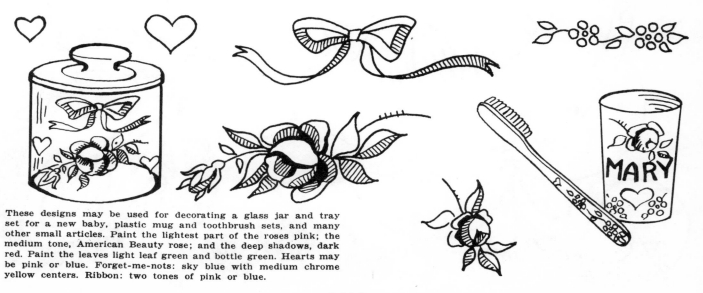

These designs may be used for decorating a glass jar and tray set for a new baby, plastic mug and toothbrush sets, and many other small articles. Paint the lightest part of the roses pink; the medium tone, American Beauty rose; and the deep shadows, dark red. Paint the leaves light leaf green and bottle green. Hearts may be pink or blue. Forget-me-nots: sky blue with medium chrome yellow centers. Ribbon: two tones of pink or blue.

BACKGROUND. Any yellow tint is good, also powder blue, gray green, stone gray, black, or contrasting dark colors.

FLOWERS. Use colors indicated.

LEAVES AND SCROLLS. Follow directions on page 53 for the coloring of the stems, leaves, and scrolls.

cobalt blue

dark blue

lemon yellow

dark blue

cobalt blue

cobalt blue

lemon yellow

vermilion

vermilion

dark leaf green

lemon yellow

dark blue

dark blue

dark blue

cobalt blue

cobalt blue

dark blue

Repeat colors for parts that are similar.

bottle green

vermilion

pink

vermilion

pink

lemon yellow

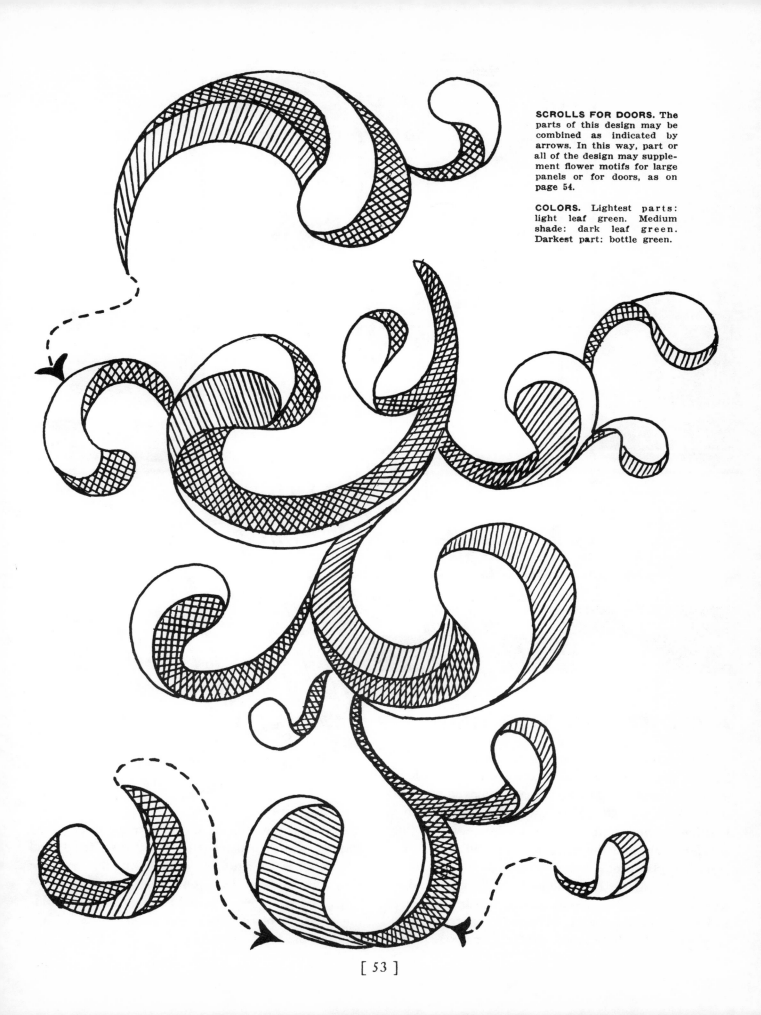

SCROLLS FOR DOORS. The parts of this design may be combined as indicated by arrows. In this way, part or all of the design may supplement flower motifs for large panels or for doors, as on page 54.

COLORS. Lightest parts: light leaf green. Medium shade: dark leaf green. Darkest part: bottle green.

A CLOSET FOR YOUR HALL

Where to hang your hat is a question in many an entrance hall. An old wardrobe solved the problem in one household. Drawers were removed, and a simple base was added to lower the whole thing. Friction catches and wooden knobs replaced the wooden latch, and the piece was well on its way to becoming glamorous.

It was placed in the center of a long wall, and a seat was built on each side. Walls, wardrobe, seats, and all other woodwork were then painted a soft gray green. The bold flower design on page 52, sup-plemented by scrolls from the patterns on pages 53 and 26, was then painted on the doors. Red tufted seat cushions repeated the color of the flowers. The back cushions were hung on the wall with tape and rings, and scrolls were painted over the screws holding them in place. Black and green linoleum was used on the floor.

WITH SAW AND SCREW DRIVER

Work for simple lines and good proportions

ONE of the important things that an art student learns is to think of basic lines and good proportions first and of details and ornamentation last. The fact that you actually can change the fundamental lines and proportions of a piece of furniture that is to be painted is one of the things that makes such a project an artistic adventure.

A good quality of enamel will cover the crudities of amateur cabinetwork and disguise the fact that different kinds of wood have been used in making alterations. A decorative design judiciously applied may accent good points, stress the length or width of the piece to give it style, or even help to cover irregularities in workmanship. Many a gayly painted flower has hidden a nailhead or hammer dent, and a painted design always breaks up surfaces so that imperfections do not show.

The more unpleasing the piece is in the beginning, the more fun it is to think out ways to improve it or turn it into something that will serve a new purpose. You will get the best effects if you allow your imagination free play. Try to think of the piece not as it is, but as you wish it could be, and the ways of making the necessary changes will suggest themselves.

If the ideas that come to you are too elaborate or too difficult to put into effect, do not dismiss them entirely. Keep right on thinking about them, but from the point of view of working out some simple version well within the ability of amateur talent. Do not get involved in details, but hold firmly to the idea of good basic lines.

Drawers are rather difficult to make and fit so that they work smoothly. Shelves, cupboards, and boxlike chests are quite easy to make. Simple bases are also easy. So the thing to do is save the drawer part of an outmoded dresser, chiffonier, sideboard, desk, or buffet, and build around it. Drawers may even be divided, as illustrated here with the old dresser that was made into two separate chests.

Shelves may be added to the top of a chest of drawers to make a break-front cupboard or at the sides to make a long low piece for a living room,

dining room, or hall. Many old tables have tops that are good, but legs or bases that are unattractive. Several suggestions are given here for changing these. A number of ways to make over outmoded beds are also outlined.

But it is not only in remodeled pieces that paint saves the day. There are simple methods of making new things of solid lumber or plywood or a combination of the two, and when they have been well sanded, painted, and decorated, they are worthy of a place of honor in any home. Elaborate cabinetwork, complicated joinings and moldings are not necessary for chests, shelves, tables, trays, boxes, and cupboards that are to be decorated. Many beautiful things may be made by selecting a painting pattern first and then planning an article to harmonize perfectly with it. A number of examples of this sort are given here.

An elaborate workshop is not necessary to do these things. It is remarkable how much may be accomplished with a hammer, a screw driver, and an ordinary handsaw. Add a brace and bit, a coping saw and a wood chisel, and you are ready to make any of the things shown here. Shaped pieces that may be cut more efficiently with a power saw may be taken to a woodworking shop after the outline is clearly marked on the stock. Clamps for holding parts while glue is drying are useful, but not essential for this kind of work. Since the piece is to be painted, brads, nails, or screws may be used in combination with glue for all joinings. The new powder type of plastic glue is quickly mixed and is even stronger than the kind that has to be heated in a gluepot. Other materials and methods that may prove useful both in altering old furniture and making new things are described here.

Plastic wood. If you are preparing a piece of furniture to be painted and then decorated, one of the new types of plastic wood now obtainable at paint stores will be an invaluable aid. You can change the location or style of old drawer pulls or handles and fill the holes and marred places with this material. Use it to fill screw holes, keyholes, cracks, or deep gouges. It is easy to mold while wet and even has been used satisfactorily to piece out broken edges, though the manufacturers do not suggest this use. When it is dry, it may be sanded smooth, and since it is mixed with water instead of oil, it does not burn through the paint and show, as putty does when used to fill holes.

Plywood. If you want to radically alter a piece of furniture, as when adding shelves to the top of an old chest of drawers or a new top to a table, plywood makes a wonderful showing with little work. When the edges have been sanded and a good enamel applied, it blends with the rest of the piece. Quarter-inch plywood is good for backings for shelves and for new bottoms in drawers. The half-inch thickness is good for light shelves. Three-quarter-inch plywood is considerably more expensive, but when painted gives the substantial effect of solid stock of the same thickness. Marine plywood should be used for outdoor pieces as it is waterproof and therefore stands the weather.

Angle irons and mending irons. Sooner or later you will want to shorten the legs of a table from the top instead of the bottom, or to fasten an old set of legs to a top section to make a table, desk, bench, or stool. A substantial job may be done quickly and easily by screwing a one-and-a-half-inch angle iron to the inside of each leg and to the underside of the top of the piece. Flat two-inch or three-inch mending irons are useful for joining the pieces of a bed head that has been cut down or for joining shelves or superstructures to chests, desks, and other pieces. Both angle and flat mending irons have innumerable uses.

Drawer pulls and handles. Plain wooden handles and drawer pulls generally are best for a painted piece of furniture. The round knob type ready to screw in place is obtainable at most hardware stores. If the piece has a modern air, three-inch or four-inch blocks of wood beveled a little at the sides make good-looking handles. These may be screwed in place from the inside of a drawer or cupboard door. Friction catches may be used for doors with wooden handles. Simple brass handles and catches may supply an interesting accent for drawers or doors, but it is always best to discard the elaborately embossed brass drawer pulls so popular a few decades ago for dressers and other pieces. New pulls frequently are all that is needed to give dignity to a set of drawers after an awkward or overelaborate mirror support

has been removed. In the kitchen, plastic handles and pulls are often considered the most practical, and a smart effect may be obtained by harmonizing their color with a painting design used for decorating.

Fake carving. Many cheap pieces of old furniture are elaborately ornamented with imitation carving that is only glued on or tacked in place with brads. Occasionally an interesting effect may be obtained by painting the carved design a contrasting color and adding flowers or ivy leaves or other motifs to elaborate on it and incorporate it in a painting design. It is best to remove the carving with a hammer and chisel or a screw driver. Be sure to rub off all traces of glue with sandpaper and fill holes with plastic wood.

Top-heavy superstructures. There was a time when most furniture was top-heavy with carving. Mirrors set in heavy scrollwork were used on top of sideboards, desks, and even bookcases. Dressers and chiffoniers were weighted down with heavy framework to hold a tipping mirror. If these superstructures are removed, there comes to light a simple piece of furniture that is perfect for decorating. The operation is quite easy to perform. Generally it consists of removing a few screws. Sometimes it is necessary to add a piece of plain molding along the back of the top of the piece to fill in a space where the superstructure was set in.

Tricks with beds. The heads of many beds of the top-heavy period were skyscraper high. In lowering these, the simplest part of the top may be replaced after sawing out a section below it, or the foot of the bed may be substituted for the head, and the old headpiece, cut off even with the top of the springs, will then become the foot and be covered with the bedspread. If both head and foot of an old wooden bed are not worth using, both may be sawed off even with the top of the springs, and a simple headpiece cut out of plywood may be screwed to the top. When the whole piece is painted and made up with a floor-length spread, the result would make Hollywood envious.

Curves for alterations. If curves are needed to take away the square look around the sides of shelves, the top of a desk, cupboard, or bed, or any other part of a piece of furniture that is being altered, you do not have to own a band saw or a jig saw in order to have them. There is sure to be a woodworking shop near by or some clever amateur fairly itching to use his power tools. All you have to do is to mark the cutting line clearly on the wood with a good black pencil, and it can be cut out for little cost. You will get especially good effects if you plan scallops and irregular edges to fit the design you wish to paint.

Legs, feet, and bases. Many outmoded pieces of furniture stand too high for present-day taste. We like tables and chairs and chests of drawers that hug the floor. Often it is possible to shorten the legs of a table by sawing them off to the right length. An old center table or even a kitchen table may be turned into a handsome coffee table this way. If the legs look sawed off, try adding round drawer-pull knobs on the bottom to make feet. Sometimes the legs or a fancy base are not the right shape to cut down. Then discard them, buy a length of curtain pole or a piece of two-by-two pine, cut new legs, add knob feet if desired, and screw the new legs in place with angle irons. Chests of drawers, old cupboards, and radio cabinets often are improved by cutting off the legs and setting the upper part on a low boxlike base that comes flush with the floor.

Your stock pile. When dismantling pieces of old furniture, save parts that look as though they might have interesting possibilities. Sometimes one bit of turning in an overelaborate set of legs may make feet or short legs for something else. Lamp bases may be made from table pedestals and fluted legs. Sections taken off old desks and sideboards may be used for wall brackets. Mirror supports sometimes may be turned around and used as supports for a shelf under a hall mirror. Curved table legs also make good console or bracket table supports. Use such pieces only if their lines are good; do not force their use just because you have them.

This low chest of drawers for a hall was made from the upper part of the old dresser shown on page 59. Two-by-four-inch blocks were used for feet, and large round drawer pulls were added. The main part of the chest was enameled dull black and decorated with pink roses traced from the pattern given here. The top was enameled white and marbled in black, gray, and pink.

Follow the color guide on page 60.

OLD AND NEW COMBINED

Multiply one old dresser by three, plus a little home carpentry, and what do you have? The answer is a handsome linen chest, a sophisticated set of drawers, and a dressing table with a graceful mirror and side brackets. The chest is shown on the opposite page, the drawers on page 57, and the dressing table on page 63. But truth to tell, it took a little more than carpentry to make these pieces what they are. The sawing and hammering produced three important pieces of furniture from one, but it was the clever and appropriate application of painting designs that made the linen chest so handsome, that gave the set of drawers an air of sophistication, and added charm to the dressing table.

The owner of this chest saw a beautifully decorated Dutch chest, with a drawer at the bottom, used as a colorful accent in a living room furnished in pieces far beyond her price limit. She went home and persuaded her husband to perform a drastic operation on the old dresser shown here. The scrollwork was removed from the bottom, and the frame of the dresser was cut in two just above the bottom drawer. A top of three-quarter-inch plywood was then cut to project one inch beyond the sides and front of this single drawer unit. A plain chest with hinged lid was made to be centered on this piece as shown in the sketch. The chest part is flush at the back, but sets in about two inches at the sides and front. When the new and old parts had been joined, new wooden pulls added to the drawers, old holes filled with plastic wood, and the whole piece smoothly sanded, it was ready for the paint.

The new drawer pulls were taken off while the front of the drawer was being enameled white, and were later painted with black enamel to match the main part of the chest. The front of the chest was enameled white first, and when dry, a stiff piece of paper was cut the shape of the panels. The black enamel was then applied around this panel pattern, as shown on page 60. The tulip designs were applied next, the one on this page being used on the drawer front, and the one on page 60 used in the panels. After the designs were dry, an antique overtone was applied to them, and then rubbed out thinly toward the edges of the panels and the drawer front.

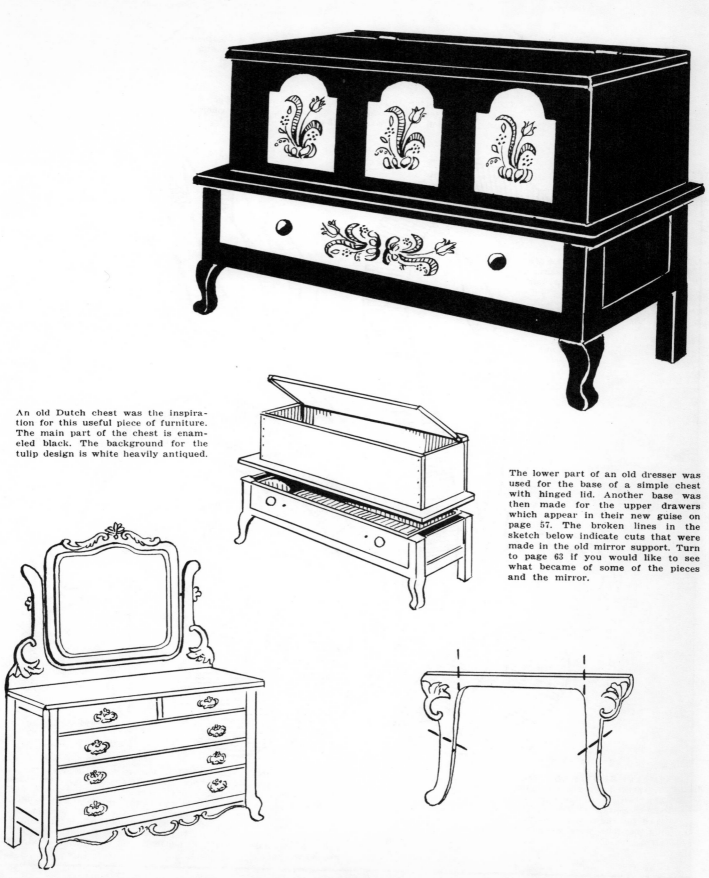

An old Dutch chest was the inspiration for this useful piece of furniture. The main part of the chest is enameled black. The background for the tulip design is white heavily antiqued.

The lower part of an old dresser was used for the base of a simple chest with hinged lid. Another base was then made for the upper drawers which appear in their new guise on page 57. The broken lines in the sketch below indicate cuts that were made in the old mirror support. Turn to page 63 if you would like to see what became of some of the pieces and the mirror.

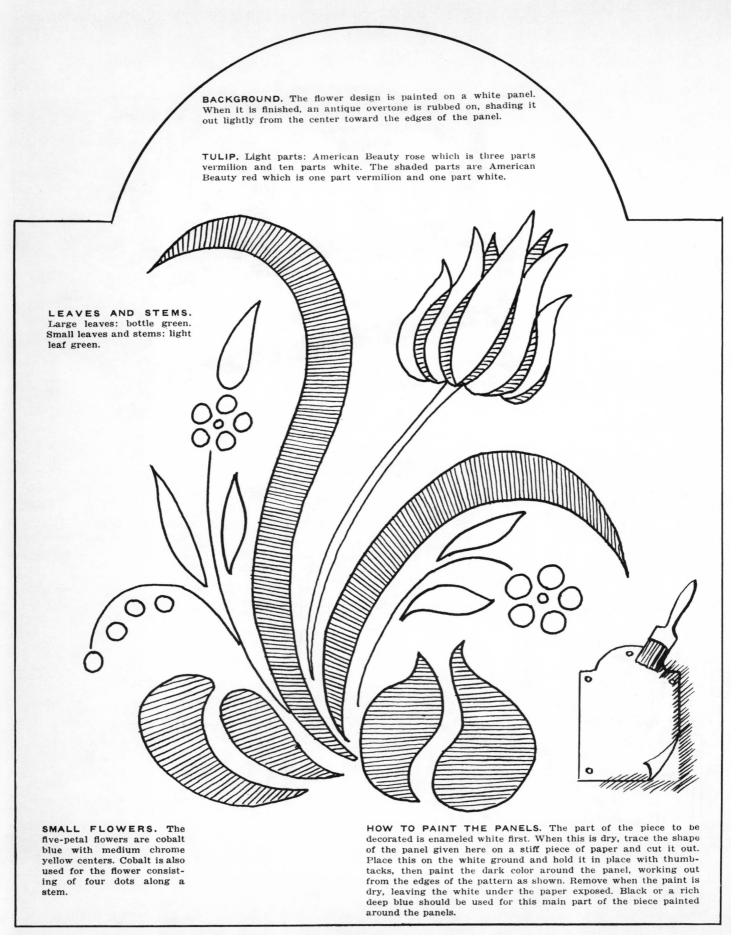

BACKGROUND. The flower design is painted on a white panel. When it is finished, an antique overtone is rubbed on, shading it out lightly from the center toward the edges of the panel.

TULIP. Light parts: American Beauty rose which is three parts vermilion and ten parts white. The shaded parts are American Beauty red which is one part vermilion and one part white.

LEAVES AND STEMS. Large leaves: bottle green. Small leaves and stems: light leaf green.

SMALL FLOWERS. The five-petal flowers are cobalt blue with medium chrome yellow centers. Cobalt is also used for the flower consisting of four dots along a stem.

HOW TO PAINT THE PANELS. The part of the piece to be decorated is enameled white first. When this is dry, trace the shape of the panel given here on a stiff piece of paper and cut it out. Place this on the white ground and hold it in place with thumbtacks, then paint the dark color around the panel, working out from the edges of the pattern as shown. Remove when the paint is dry, leaving the white under the paper exposed. Black or a rich deep blue should be used for this main part of the piece painted around the panels.

LEAF SPRAYS. These designs may be used as separate units, or they may supplement other designs. Parts of the large spray may be used to fill spaces of different sizes and shapes.

LEAVES. Effective painted entirely in dark leaf green, or lighter greens may be used toward the tips of sprays.

BACKGROUND. Good on ivory, cream, olive, gray green or lacquer red. These sprays are sometimes painted in gold on a bottle green or black ground.

Pattern for cornice at top of shadow boxes on page 32.

HEART. The heart in the center of the cornice pattern is American vermilion.

REVERSING DESIGNS. See directions for transferring designs.

[61]

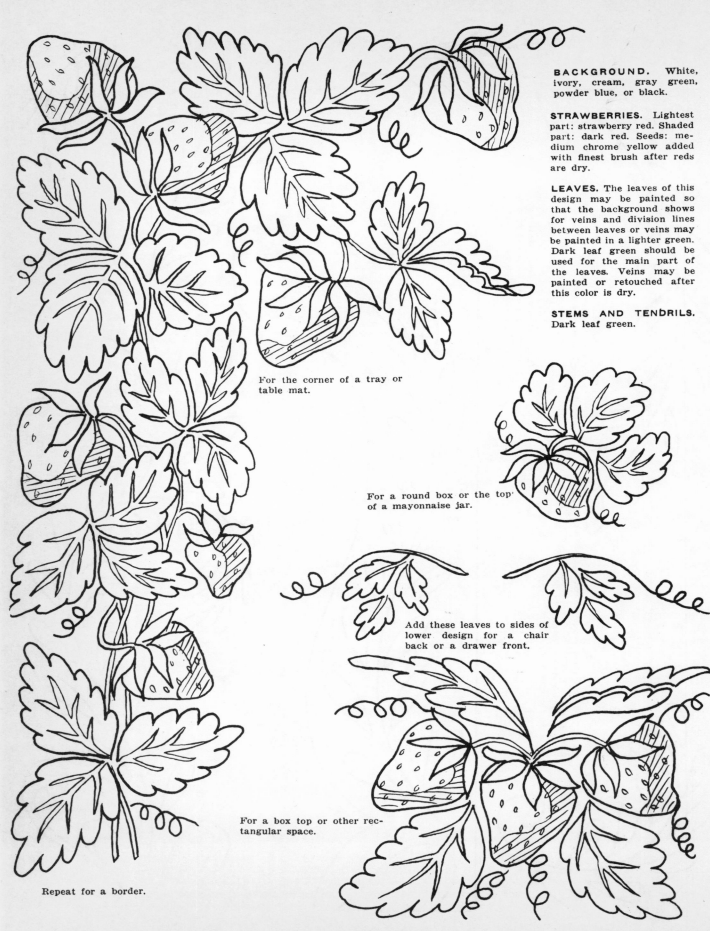

BACKGROUND. White, ivory, cream, gray green, powder blue, or black.

STRAWBERRIES. Lightest part: strawberry red. Shaded part: dark red. Seeds: medium chrome yellow added with finest brush after reds are dry.

LEAVES. The leaves of this design may be painted so that the background shows for veins and division lines between leaves or veins may be painted in a lighter green. Dark leaf green should be used for the main part of the leaves. Veins may be painted or retouched after this color is dry.

STEMS AND TENDRILS. Dark leaf green.

For the corner of a tray or table mat.

For a round box or the top of a mayonnaise jar.

Add these leaves to sides of lower design for a chair back or a drawer front.

For a box top or other rectangular space.

Repeat for a border.

THE SKIRTS ARE PAINTED TOO

This is a strawberry-sundae vanity table, the kind that any girl loves to concoct from odds and ends of things on hand. The deep turquoise-blue velvet ribbon used as a note of contrast is the only new item purchased here. The mirror and side brackets will be recognized immediately as salvage from the old dresser shown on page 59.

Mirror frame, brackets, and an old table were all painted white. The table was decorated, and then a medium dark antique overtone was applied. In the rubbing process, only a little of the antique mixture

was removed from the crevices of carving. This was done with a dry brush. The carving was further emphasized by turning the mirror upside down, thus relating it more closely to the table and the brackets.

The stool is a disguised butter tub, and the skirts are the best parts of old sheets with strawberries from the pattern on the opposite page painted at more or less regularly spaced points. The pair of boxes on the brackets is decorated with a small version of the design on page 95, which shows a man presenting a demure lady with a rose.

SALVAGING GOOD MATERIAL

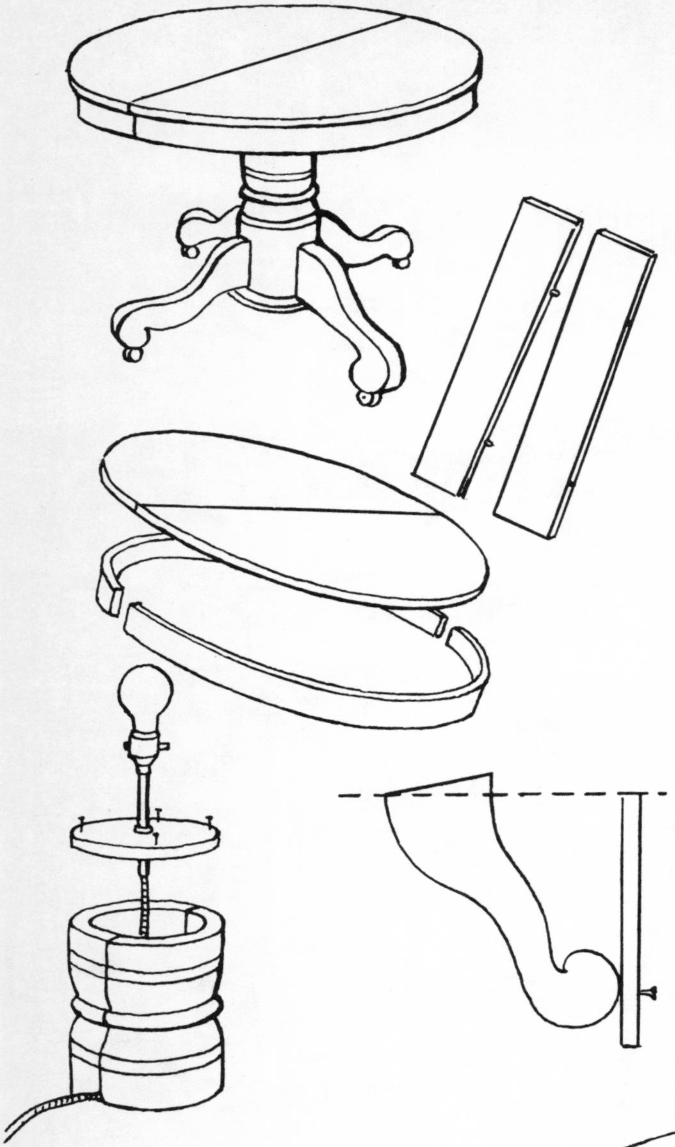

It takes time to season lumber, and any smooth well-seasoned piece is valuable whether you find it in a lumberyard or in your own stock pile. Take a second look at any piece of furniture that does not exactly suit your taste. Perhaps it may be broken down and good material reused in some entirely new way. If you are not equipped to do this yourself, it is often worth while to have it done at a woodworking shop.

A number of things were made from the old golden oak table shown here, and none has any resemblance to the original piece. The lamp base made from the pedestal is the one used on the step table on page 18. The legs of the table were turned into brackets. Two of them are combined with extra leaves to make the console shown on page 15.

The low table for a boy's room, a recreation room, or other informal room shows an application of the cowboy design on the opposite page. After the original finish had been removed, the design was painted over one coat of clear varnish on the natural wood. After the table was decorated, more coats of varnish were added to build up a hard finish. As golden oak is inclined to blister when paint is applied, it is best to remove the original finish.

The rim from the top of the old dining table makes the legs of this coffee table. The rope design from the opposite page is painted on the legs, and the cowboy's rope may be made to spell out in bold handwriting any appropriate legend one likes.

the skies are not cloudy all day

BACKGROUND. Cream color with bottle green ground line.

HORSE. Body white with tan shadows. Mane and tail: tan with medium brown shadows. Hoofs, eye, nostril, and mouth: dark brown. Bridle: dark brown. Saddle: tan with medium brown edge.

COWBOY. Flesh: sun tan. Eye and hair: dark brown. Mouth: vermilion. Hat: tan with medium brown shadows and dark brown band. Vest: tan. Bandanna: vermilion. Shirt: cobalt blue and vermilion. Trousers: cobalt blue with dark blue shadows. Boot: dark brown with tan stirrup. Lariat: medium brown.

ROPE DESIGN. Light part of twist: tan. Dark part: medium brown.

ROSES. Lightest part of the two large roses and all buds: dark coral. Medium shade: vermilion. Darkest part: dark red. Lightest part of small rose: light chrome yellow. Medium shade: chrome yellow. Darkest part: burnt orange.

TULIP. Lightest part: chrome yellow. Medium shading: orange. Darkest part: burnt orange.

BLUEBELLS. Side petals: cobalt blue. Center petal: light cobalt.

LILIES OF THE VALLEY. White shading to ivory toward end of stem.

ANEMONES. White with brassy yellow centers.

MORNING-GLORIES. Medium cobalt blue with ivory throats with cobalt blue lines.

BACKGROUND. Cream or black.

GREEN COLORING. Parts of leaves, stems, and calyx left white in the pattern are to be painted mustard green. Parts with medium shading: olive green. Darkest shading: moss green. Tendrils: mustard green.

SCROLLS. Light lemon yellow. May be shaded with lemon yellow and olive green.

DESIGN MAY BE USED FOR CHAIR BACKS OR TRAYS.

[66]

THE FINAL FINISH

How to use antique overtones and dull or glossy varnish

IF YOU WANT to give richness and depth of tone to the things you decorate, a final surface finish is necessary. This must be applied after the paint is thoroughly dry and hard. There are a number of different treatments that may be used for different purposes and to give different effects. A high-quality clear uncolored waterproof varnish gives painted articles a hard surface that withstands wear and may be washed frequently. It also protects clothing from colors that have a tendency to rub off, as is sometimes the case with decorated chairs. Waterproof varnish is especially important for hand-decorated trays and table tops, and for boxes and other small articles that are handled a great deal. This does not mean that every piece must have a high gloss. A semigloss or mat-finish varnish may be used, or an even softer effect may be obtained by using the rubbed finish described here.

An antique finish. The purpose of an antique finish is not to make something look old that is not old, as is popularly supposed. The fact is that the artists who decorated antique painted furniture and other objects as well as those who painted landscapes and portraits, a hundred years or more ago, often treated the finished pieces with an overtone usually of raw umber or raw sienna mixed with turpentine and varnish. The purpose of this was to pull the colors together in tone by placing one tone over all, and to give them all richness by slightly dulling their brilliance. Antique overtones are applied to things we paint today for exactly the same reason. We also rub highlights in the overtone to give variety to the surface just as they did. But today we often carry this idea a step farther by tinting the overtone a special color to harmonize with the predominant color in the room in which the article is to be used. You will be surprised at how easy it is to use this method to soften down colors and give a painted object exactly the value you want it to have in a room. Since the overtone may be rubbed off easily while it is wet, it is possible to experiment as much as you like until you have just the effect you want. In this way many a painted article that has seemed garish and crude has been turned into something with beautiful muted colorings blending into its surroundings.

Colors used for overtones. Umber and sienna are the two pigments that traditionally have been used for overtones because of their transparent quality. Raw umber is a grayish greenish brown color. Burnt umber is almost chocolate brown. The best quality of umber comes from the island of Cyprus, is marketed through the port of Constantinople, and is therefore called Turkey umber. Raw sienna is a dull yellow color about like yellow ochre but clear and transparent. It is the base for many cream and tan tones. Burnt sienna is a brownish red. These two pigments, raw or burnt, diluted more or less with a mixing medium, give you a good range from which to choose suitable overtone colors—all with a brownish cast. Raw Turkey umber is the most useful of the group, as it is light enough to be tinted with any color or mixture of colors that you may want to use and it still keeps its transparency even though considerably more opaque color is added. Black or very dark brown is often added to raw umber to make the overtone for something with a red background.

How to mix overtones. Six tablespoons of overtone mixture will do a chair or other small piece of furniture. However, the mixture will keep in a tight screw-top jar, so it does not matter if you mix a little too much. The following recipe makes a good basic mixture to which black or color may be added as desired. If a light overtone is wanted, use less of the raw umber.

Recipe for medium dark overtone

2 tablespoons raw Turkey umber
3 tablespoons turpentine
1 tablespoon clear waterproof varnish

Squeeze the umber into a jar. Add the turpentine and mix it with your brush. Add the varnish last and mix thoroughly. If you increase or decrease the amount, be sure to keep the same proportions. If a very large panel, door, or table top is to be done at one time, add a drop or two of linseed oil to the mixture to keep it from drying too fast.

How to apply the overtone. It is essential that the painted surface is dry and hard before the overtone is applied. Most artists apply a coat of clear varnish over the paint and allow it to dry before applying the overtone. This fixes the colors so there is no possibility of their being smudged when rubbing on the overtone. Apply the overtone with your regular varnish brush. For small objects, the entire surface may be covered at one time. For larger pieces, do one section at a time, completing each drawer front, the side, top, or panels separately. Brush the overtone into the depressions of carved parts. Now wad a soft clean cloth and start to rub off the overtone with a circular motion. Work for a slightly mottled effect with the dark tone left in cracks and depressions. The center part of a top or panel is usually rubbed lighter than the edges. After rubbing lightly, the darker parts may be blended into the lighter with a dry brush. For all informal pieces of the provincial type, the blending should be very casual with streaks and irregularities plainly showing. The overtone for formal furniture is blended more evenly.

Final varnishing. One or more coats of either mat-finish or high-gloss varnish applied after the overtone is dry gives a rich surface texture. It also prevents the overtone from rubbing off and that is essential for chairs and seats and for trays and table tops. Always use clear waterproof varnish and let it flow on evenly, spreading it with the brush quickly, a small section at a time. Never go back and brush over the surface, as varnish starts to harden almost immediately and brush marks are sure to show. Any number of coats of varnish may be applied if you let each one get perfectly dry before the next is put on. Fifteen or twenty coats are sometimes used to give a lacquer effect.

A rubbed finish. After a coat of varnish is very hard it may be rubbed with fine steel wool or sandpaper to give a satin-smooth but slightly dull surface. Each successive coat of a heavy high-gloss varnish may be rubbed in this manner to build up a beautiful hard finish and to smooth out slight irregularities. The final coat then may be rubbed with a soft rag dipped in oil and then in powdered pumice, which may be obtained by the ounce at any drugstore. If you paint a piece that you like, you will enjoy taking special care with the finish.

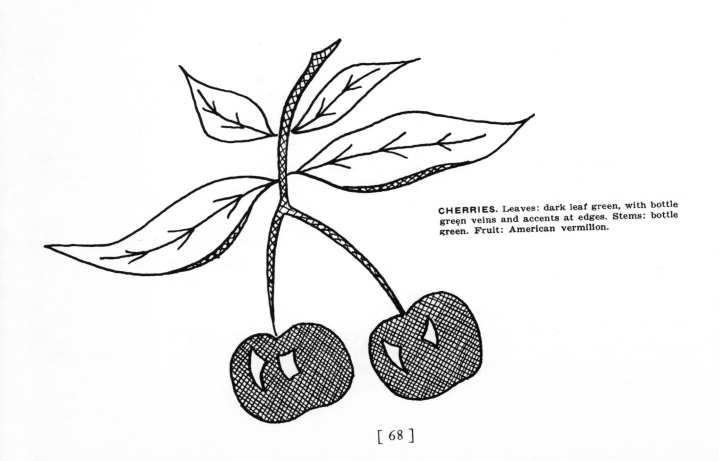

CHERRIES. Leaves: dark leaf green, with bottle green veins and accents at edges. Stems: bottle green. Fruit: American vermilion.

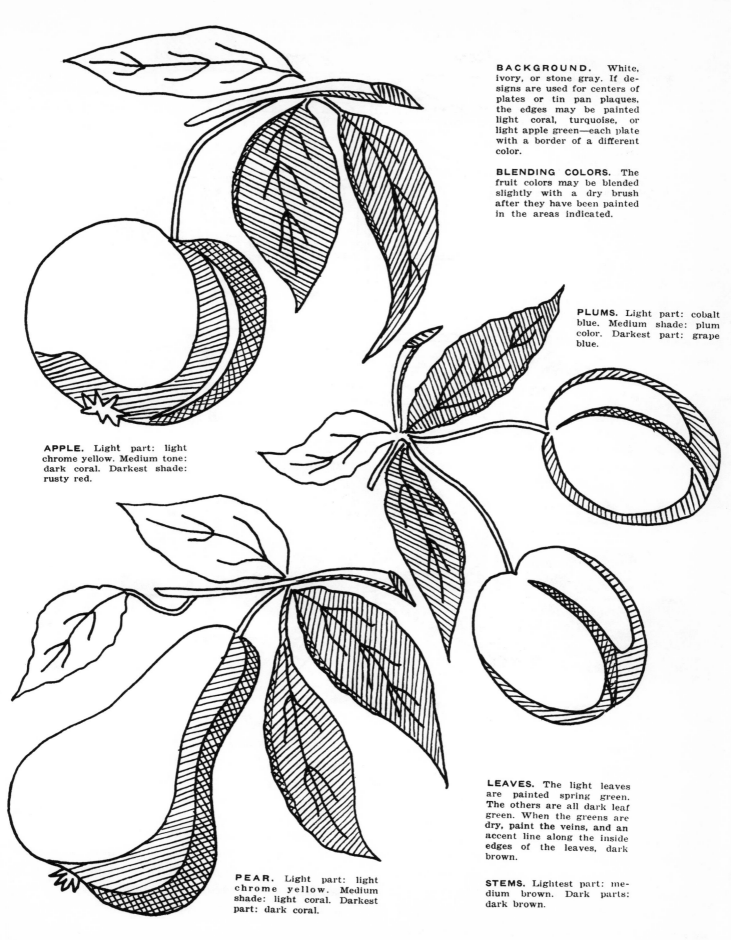

BACKGROUND. White, ivory, or stone gray. If designs are used for centers of plates or tin pan plaques, the edges may be painted light coral, turquoise, or light apple green—each plate with a border of a different color.

BLENDING COLORS. The fruit colors may be blended slightly with a dry brush after they have been painted in the areas indicated.

PLUMS. Light part: cobalt blue. Medium shade: plum color. Darkest part: grape blue.

APPLE. Light part: light chrome yellow. Medium tone: dark coral. Darkest shade: rusty red.

LEAVES. The light leaves are painted spring green. The others are all dark leaf green. When the greens are dry, paint the veins, and an accent line along the inside edges of the leaves, dark brown.

STEMS. Lightest part: medium brown. Dark parts: dark brown.

PEAR. Light part: light chrome yellow. Medium shade: light coral. Darkest part: dark coral.

[69]

GAY GARDEN FLOWER DESIGNS

On the opposite page and the following pages is a series of flower patterns which are so adaptable that you will find uses for them wherever gay colors are needed to brighten an informal spot. These designs are based on simplified flower forms that have become traditional in the folk art of many countries. The motifs are drawn here in such a way that they may be used singly or be fitted together to form borders or large panels.

The dinette shown here gives clear evidence of how these motifs may be used to add interest to a corner that would otherwise be dull and commonplace. The blinds, made of three-quarter-inch plywood, are painted on both sides. When they are closed the room is still full of color and cheer.

Bows for the ruffled curtains, the chair seat cushions, table mats, and floor linoleum all pick up and repeat the clear blues in the flowers. A color scheme featuring greens, reds, or yellows is just as satisfactory with these multicolored posies. It is easy to plan a new room around them or fit them into an old one.

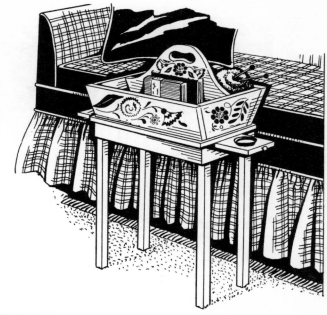

FOR THE
HANDY MAN TO MAKE

If there is a basement workshop in your home and a handy man with enthusiasm about using power tools, here are three attractive projects to make and decorate. The clothes hamper made of quarter-inch plywood may be planned to fit in any odd space in bathroom, hall, or bedroom. The old-fashioned knife box may hold books, handwork, and other odds and ends, or it may be used for serving drinks at parties. The spice chest would be useful in any kitchen.

The garden flower patterns on pages 72 through 76 are used for all three of the articles shown here. Heart and flower designs would also be appropriate. The strawberry designs would fit the knife box especially well. The large bird design on page 31 would make a striking motif for the front of a clothes hamper similar to this one. Trailing sprays of ivy would be good for any of these pieces. A knife box or a spice chest is especially attractive if the design is painted on the natural wood background. One coat of shellac may be applied and rubbed with fine sandpaper before the decorating is done. After the design has been painted, the piece may be varnished and then rubbed down to dull the high gloss.

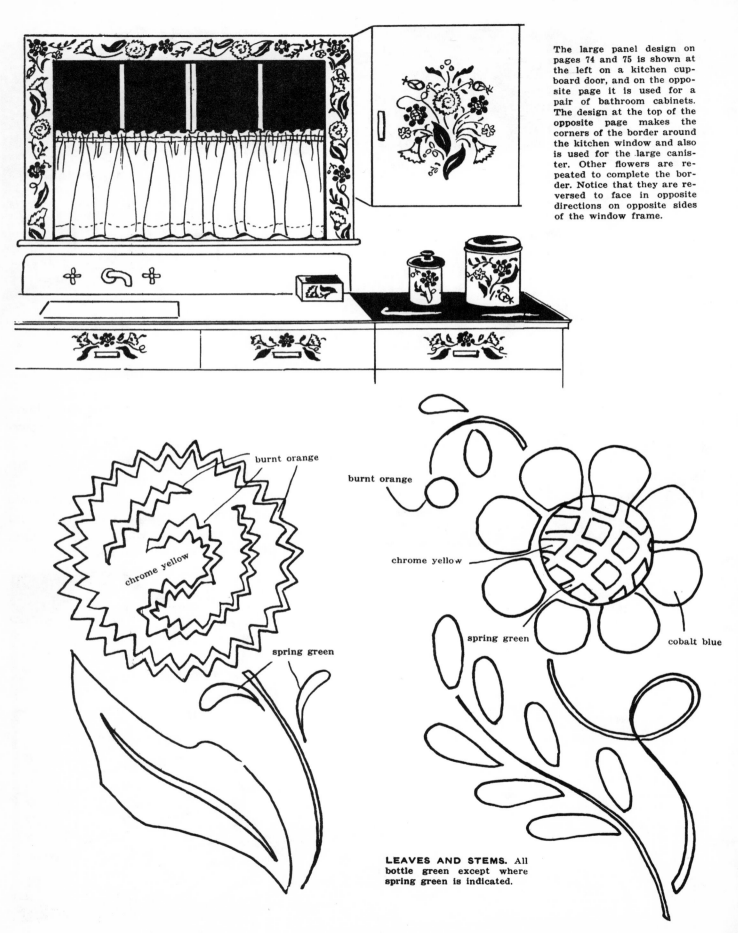

The large panel design on pages 74 and 75 is shown at the left on a kitchen cupboard door, and on the opposite page it is used for a pair of bathroom cabinets. The design at the top of the opposite page makes the corners of the border around the kitchen window and also is used for the large canister. Other flowers are repeated to complete the border. Notice that they are reversed to face in opposite directions on opposite sides of the window frame.

burnt orange

chrome yellow

spring green

burnt orange

chrome yellow

spring green

cobalt blue

LEAVES AND STEMS. All bottle green except where spring green is indicated.

LEAVES AND STEMS. All
bottle green except where
spring green is indicated.

spring green

cobalt blue

chrome yellow

spring green

spring green

spring green

Repeat colors for parts that are similar.

cobalt blue

FIRST AID

FORMULA

spring green

spring green

bottle green

spring green

burnt orange

chrome yellow

burnt orange

chrome yellow

spring green

burnt orange

chrome yellow

bottle green

chrome yellow

cobalt blue

LEAVES AND STEMS. All bottle green except where spring green is indicated.

Repeat colors for parts that are similar.

BACKGROUND. White, ivory, cream, or gray.

BROKEN LINES. Used to indicate where this motif joins the one on the opposite page.

burnt orange

chrome yellow

burnt orange

chrome yellow

spring green

spring green

spring green

chrome yellow

spring green

spring green

burnt orange

spring green

spring green

chrome yellow

chrome yellow

bottle green

spring green

burnt orange

burnt orange

burnt orange

spring green

chrome yellow

spring green

cobalt blue

BROKEN LINES. Used to indicate where this motif joins the one on the opposite page.

Repeat colors for parts that are similar.

spring green

spring green

spring green

spring green

spring green

spring green

pink

pink

pink

chrome yellow

cobalt blue

bottle green

burnt orange

chrome yellow

chrome yellow

[75]

Repeat colors for parts that are similar.

spring green

burnt orange

chrome yellow

chrome yellow

spring green

bottle green

hrome yellow

burnt orange

chrome yellow

burnt orange

chrome yellow

spring green

cobalt blue

LEAVES AND STEMS. All bottle green except where spring green is indicated.

cobalt blue

spring green

burnt orange

chrome yellow

spring green

burnt orange

cobalt blue

chrome yellow

spring green

burnt orange

spring green

NEAT AND NAUTICAL

This simple sea chest shows just one of many ways that anchors, rope knots, and ships may be used in decorating things for a boy's room, a recreation room, or a summer cottage at the shore. The large ship design may be painted directly on a wall over a mantel, or a striking picture may be made of it by painting it on paper in water color and then mounting it with a wide white mat. It, as well as the anchor and rope, will also be useful for decorating cupboard doors, wastebaskets, hampers, wood boxes, magazine racks, and many other things.

The small versions of these designs may be used for chair backs, small boxes, lamp shades, or any object that you wish to give the flavor of the sea. If you like ships, you may even want to use one of the smaller designs for greeting cards. They are easy to paint, especially if you outline the ropes and ladders for the small designs with pen and ink instead of a brush. The blue of sky and water may be blended into any background, as explained in the directions with the large ship pattern.

This sea chest is painted brown and decorated with the ship, anchor and rope designs on pages 78 and 79.

SKY AND WATER. Paint the entire portion to be sky and water sky blue, and let this color dry before transferring the design. If the ship is to be painted on a chest that is some other color, blend the light blue sky and water with a dry brush around the edges so that it fades into the color of the chest. When the design has been transferred, paint the curling waves next to the ship white. The shaded part of the water is deep sea blue.

SHIP. Brownish black next to water. Upper part of hull: gun-metal gray. Masts: golden tan. Rigging and rope ladders: brownish black. Sails: white with shaded part silver gray. Wind stocking at top: brownish black. Flag: vermilion red, white, and flag blue. Lower flag: flag blue.

BACKGROUND. These designs and the ship design will show up to best advantage on chests and other furnishings painted a dark color, such as flag or deep sea blue, bottle green, or dark brown.

ANCHOR AND CHAIN. Silver gray with brownish black for the dark parts.

KNOTTED ROPE. Silver gray with twist shadows brownish black.

MELON PEDDLER AND PALM TREE. This amusing picture may be painted on blocks of wood to be used as hot dish mats or simulated tiles to hang on the wall. It is also shown on the opposite page combined with a green saw-tooth border for a place mat of oilcloth or heavily varnished composition board.

BACKGROUND. The whole background for the picture is a plain warm cream color. This should be painted first and allowed to dry before the design is traced.

PALM TREE. Paint the light side of the trunk golden tan and the dark side dark brown. The medium tone is a blend of these two. The leaves should be painted light leaf green with dark leaf green shadows.

CART. Terra-cotta red with dark red shadows and outlining for the wheel. The melons are spring green striped with bottle green. Sales ticket: white with brown writing and stick.

MAN. Flesh: sun tan. Neck and hand at side of face slightly darker. Hair and eyes: brownish black. Mouth: red. Hat: medium chrome yellow with golden tan shadows, and terra-cotta red edge for brim. Paint the shirt white and let dry before adding terra-cotta red and peacock blue plaid and a gray shadow. Trousers: peacock blue with darker blue shadows. Shoes: medium brown. Box seat: medium chrome yellow.

GARLAND. This decoration may be used for walls, furniture, trays, and many other articles. The garland may be made longer by repeating parts of it.

Starting at the top, the colors for the garland are as follows. Nailhead: chartreuse. Ribbon and stems: light and dark leaf green. Light side of first large pepper: flamingo red. Dark side: dark red with the medium tone a blend of the two. First pair of small peppers: peacock blue with dark blue dots. Second large pepper: chartreuse with olive green shadow, and medium tone a blend of the two. Second pair of small peppers: medium chrome yellow with burnt orange stripes. Flowers: flamingo red. Large pepper at bottom: terra-cotta red with dark red shadow blended in and medium chrome yellow streaks near bottom. All leaves are light and dark leaf green.

SOUTH OF THE BORDER

It is fun to paint the Mexican designs which follow, and you will find many uses for them. Why not have a Mexican corner for informal meals and for the children to use for study or games? The space may be partitioned off, or its boundaries may be marked with brightly painted moldings. Lattice strips painted green are used to frame the corner shown here. Table and chairs are also painted this color. The seat is upholstered in red leatherette which also is used in strips folded and glued double for woven chair seats.

Garlands of dried peppers and flowers are painted on the wall, and blocks of wood are painted like Mexican tiles and hung in a straight row. Chairs and table mats, wooden coasters and hot dish mats, trays and even the baby's bib and high-chair mat are painted in gay Mexican designs.

SERENADER. This figure, combined with a border of wavy lines and dots in green and orange, is used to decorate a tray in the group of objects shown on page 81. He also appears on one of the wall tiles.

NOTE. Clear definition of all details is important in painting all of these Mexican figures. Good sharp-pointed brushes are essential. Avoid using much paint on your brush at one time. If colors run together and blur the edges, let the paint dry before proceeding with the finishing touches.

BACKGROUND. Here again plain cream color is used for the entire background. Coloring for palm tree and cactus, same as indicated elsewhere in this series. Shadows indicating steps, tan.

MAN. Flesh: sun tan. Eye: black. Hat: medium chrome yellow with golden tan shadows, and green brim edging and chin band. Scarf: burnt orange with tan shadows, green bands and fringe, and peacock blue dots. Suit: peacock blue with dark blue shadows and burnt orange and green trimming. Shoes: black. Guitar: golden tan for front, tan sides with medium brown shadows, black strings and other details.

MEXICAN HAT. This motif, as well as the hen and cock on the following page and the flowering cactus, is attractive painted on coasters of wood or glass. Perhaps you have a set of old coasters that may be repainted and then varnished with moisture-resistant varnish. Pieces of ordinary window glass may be cut in small squares, edges ground smooth, and then painted to make coasters. The hat stands out sharply if painted medium chrome yellow with golden tan shadows, green and red trimming around brim, and two tones of green for ties.

GIRL WITH FRUIT AND PITCHER. Another of the Mexican series that will add a bright note to decorations for a south-of-the-border kitchen, dinette, recreation room, or sun porch.

BACKGROUND. Paint the whole piece plain cream color first, and allow to dry. Bars for window are gray. Dark shadow at side of window: medium brown. Bottom of window: tan. Light leaf green at base of building and for leaves of vine. Main stem of vine: medium brown. Flowers: flamingo red.

GIRL. Flesh: sun tan. Hair: brownish black with flamingo red bow. Bowl on head: medium brown with dark brown shadows. Pineapples: golden tan with brown outlining and green leaves. Other fruit: lemon yellow and orange. Bodice: white with light blue shadows and cuff. Skirt: white with light leaf green stripes and orange dots. Pitcher: tan with brown shadow, and green and red decoration. Shoes: medium brown.

HEN. Body: medium brown with dark brown feather outlines. Neck and top of wing: golden tan. Tail and wing feathers: greenish black. Comb: vermilion. Eye: dark brown. Bill and feet: lemon yellow.

COCK. Body: golden tan. Top of wing and breast, orange. Head and base tail feathers: greenish black. Wing feathers and top of tail: bottle green. Comb: vermilion. Bill and feet: lemon yellow. Eye: black and white.

FLOWER VENDOR. Like all the other figures in this series, this man with his picturesque load of bright posies may be used to decorate simulated tiles, table mats, trays, cupboard doors, and furniture.

BACKGROUND. The background should be painted first and allowed to dry before the design is transferred to it. A plain tone of cream color is used for the entire piece. The ground line and plants are cactus green with bottle green shadows and details.

MAN. Flesh: sun tan. Hair and eye: brownish black. Hat: medium chrome yellow with golden tan shadow. Brim trimming and ties: flamingo red. Suit: peacock blue with dark blue shadows. Shoes: medium brown. Basket: medium chrome yellow, with tan outlining the band around the basket, olive green. Flowers: turquoise blue and flamingo red with yellow centers.

CACTUS MOTIF. This little design may be used for coasters and to decorate odd corners. It is most effective if the center portion of the plant is painted cactus green, with side shoots light leaf green, and shadow and spines bottle green. Buds and flower: flamingo with dark red shadow.

DONKEY. This playful animal may have any number of applications. He seems especially appropriate for the high-chair place mat and bib set shown on page 81. He might even be painted right on the high chair. Grownups will like him just as much as children if you paint him on their place mats. Paint the main part of the body taupe gray, with white for nose, spot on head, neck, stomach, and end of tail. Mane, feet, and ear shadow: brownish black. Eye: black and white. Saddle: peacock blue. Briddle, reins, and belly-band: vermilion.

BACKGROUND. The whole background may be cream color, or the sky may be painted turquoise blue. Cactus: same as indicated for similar motifs in this series.

PIG AND CACTUS. This spotted porker may be painted on the usual cream ground, or on turquoise, or on any other blue or yellow. He is white with medium brown spots, shadows, and outlining. Snoot, eye, and feet: black. Cactus plant: cactus green with bottle green for lines and blades of grass.

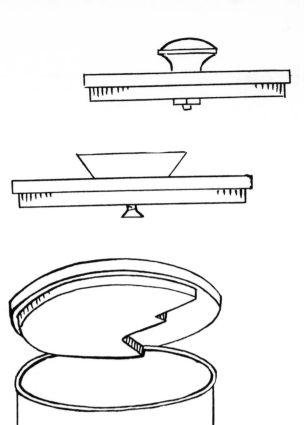

CORNUCOPIA DESIGN. Background: gray green. Light parts of side and end designs and the cornucopia: lemon yellow. Dark parts: olive brown. Light parts of leaves: spring green. Dark parts: dark leaf green. Grapes: cobalt blue with grape blue shadows.

SWIRL DESIGN. Background: gray green or cream. Top and bottom: lacquer red edged with chrome yellow. Swirls: lacquer red with chrome yellow centers. Knob for top: brass or painted chrome yellow.

BOXES FROM OLD TIN CANS

What did you do with the meat or fish tin you opened the other day? What became of that cunning little round one that your new can opener cut with such a smooth edge? Don't search the city dump, but do save them next time. See those smart-looking lids sketched above? They may be made to fit any can so that it immediately becomes a box or a canister.

The lids are made of two pieces of quarter-inch plywood. One piece is cut a little smaller than the top of the can so that it will fit inside. The other piece is a little larger so that it rests on the edge of the can. The two are glued together, and there you have a nice snug lid. A small knob may be added,

ROUND BOX OR CANISTER. Small tin cans fitted with wooden lids make attractive cigarette boxes. Larger cans make tea caddies or canisters.

FLAT TIN BOX. Small flat cans with wooden lids make good cigarette boxes, or they may be decorated to make stamp boxes for a desk.

IVY FOR A SMALL BOX. Background: lacquer red or gray green. Large leaves and stems: dark leaf green. Small leaves: spring green. Vines: bottle green. Scroll border: lemon yellow. Repeat single spray around sides.

LEAF BORDER FOR SIDES. Repeat this spray spaced evenly around the sides of the box. Paint entirely in bottle green.

as shown, or a wooden handle, cut out of a small block of wood, may be screwed in place. Knobs and handles are not really essential, but they do lend style sometimes, especially to tall canisters and tea caddies.

Large cans gayly decorated with the contents indicated either in simple lettering or script serve many uses in the kitchen. Why not have a shelf of them for things other than foods? Nails, screws, washers, and other gadgets and widgets might just as well have an attractive home in some handy spot as on a dusty bench in the basement. Just find someone with a jig saw to cut out lids, and you will soon have enough tin boxes to keep you busy painting for a long time. You will be surprised at how interesting the lines and proportions of many of them are.

DUTCH ROSE DESIGN. Background: powder blue or cream. Rose: ashes of roses with wine red outlines and shadows. Jar: bottle green with lemon yellow cross marks and handles. Leaves: bottle green and light leaf green. Small flowers: outlined in ashes of roses with wine red dots in center. Side sprays: bottle green with lemon yellow tips.

ROUND TRINKET BOX. Salmon cans and other flat tin cans fitted with wooden lids make useful desk boxes for paper clips and odds and ends, also boxes for jewelry and trinkets.

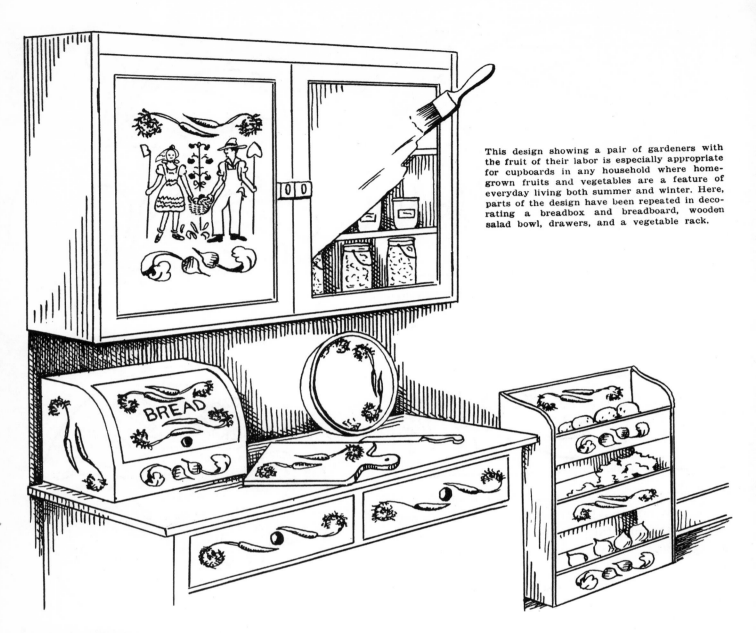

This design showing a pair of gardeners with the fruit of their labor is especially appropriate for cupboards in any household where home-grown fruits and vegetables are a feature of everyday living both summer and winter. Here, parts of the design have been repeated in decorating a breadbox and breadboard, wooden salad bowl, drawers, and a vegetable rack.

PAINTED GLASS DOORS

If you need every inch of cupboard space for storing things that are not particularly sightly, it is possible to paint glass doors to make them opaque. They may then be decorated just as though they were made of wood or metal. Most enamels adhere to glass. Avoid using paint that has been thinned much with oil. A little varnish added to flat paint will make it more adhesive, though it will add gloss.

It is also possible to decorate glass from the underside. This is very effective, but it means that the design must be painted first without overlapping the colors. Anything painted on top of the first color put down will not show from the outside. The background is then painted last after the design is dry.

COLOR GUIDE FOR DESIGN ON OPPOSITE PAGE.

CARROTS. Lightest part: carrot yellow. Shaded part: burnt orange. Stems and leaves: spring green.

WOMAN. Flesh: sun tan. Dark coral cheeks. Vermilion lips. Outlines of nose, eyebrows, and lashes: medium brown. Hair and eyes: any color preferred. Kerchief: vermilion and white. Bodice: white with apple green shadows. Dress: apple green trimmed in white. Socks: vermilion. Shoes: brownish black. Hoe: gun-metal gray with orange handle.

TOMATO VINE. Stake: orange. Stems and leaves: light leaf green. Base leaves: dark leaf green. Ties: lemon yellow. Tomatoes: tomato red.

BASKET. Straw: lemon yellow. Tomatoes: tomato red. Melon: gray green striped with moss green.

MAN. Hat: lemon yellow with medium brown band. Flesh: sun tan. Cheeks: dark coral. Lips: vermilion. Eyes and hair: any color desired. Shirt: white with powder blue shadows. Overalls: cobalt blue. Handkerchief: vermilion. Shoes: brownish black. Spade: gun metal with orange handle.

TURNIPS. Lightest part of leaves: light leaf green. Shaded part: bottle green. Darkest part of turnip: plum color. Medium tone: heliotrope. Lightest part: white.

COLOR GUIDE ON OPPOSITE PAGE.

BACKGROUND. Deep cream or gray.

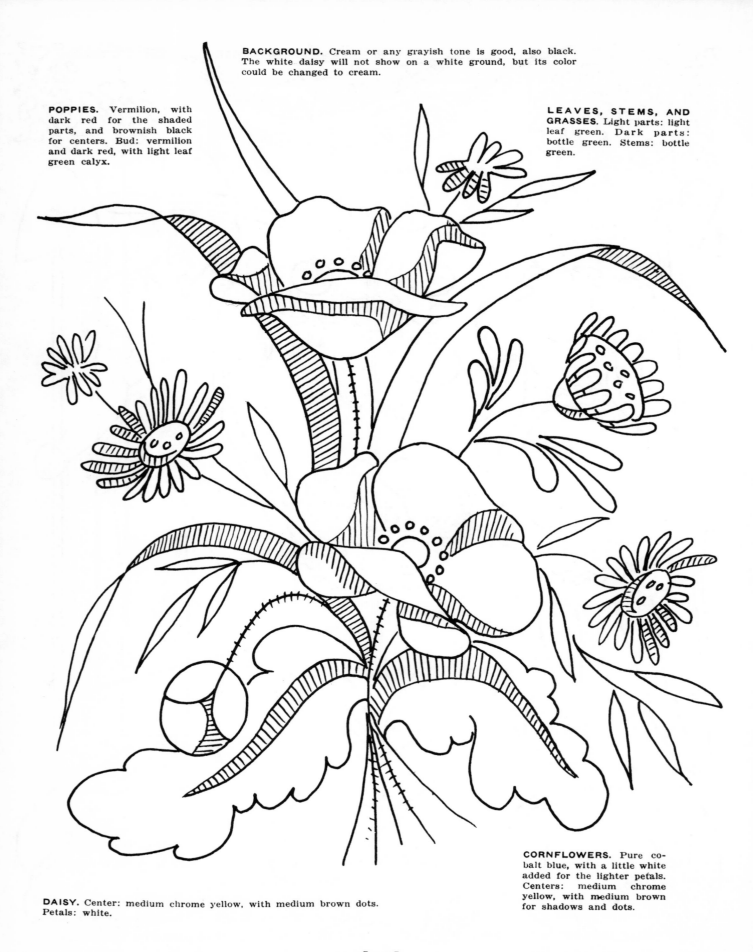

BACKGROUND. Cream or any grayish tone is good, also black. The white daisy will not show on a white ground, but its color could be changed to cream.

POPPIES. Vermilion, with dark red for the shaded parts, and brownish black for centers. Bud: vermilion and dark red, with light leaf green calyx.

LEAVES, STEMS, AND GRASSES. Light parts: light leaf green. Dark parts: bottle green. Stems: bottle green.

CORNFLOWERS. Pure cobalt blue, with a little white added for the lighter petals. Centers: medium chrome yellow, with medium brown for shadows and dots.

DAISY. Center: medium chrome yellow, with medium brown dots. Petals: white.

SHUTTING OUT A VIEW

With every inch of a house in use and the living room doing double duty as a guest room, glass doors are not as satisfactory as in the days of more spacious living. Curtains over them are a makeshift and give no real feeling of privacy, but the doors shown here prove that paint cleverly used may be both decorative and practical.

When they are open, the lovely colors of the designs in alternate panels are in the living room though they show from the hall. A different method was used here than either of the two described for painting glass cupboard doors. These doors were painted all over from the living room side first in ivory to match the room woodwork. The designs were then painted directly on the glass from the hall side, the plain paint on the back showing through and giving the effect of glazed tile.

At the sides of the doors are wooden racks painted in the strawberry design and heavily antiqued. These were made to fit tin bread pans which hold vines.

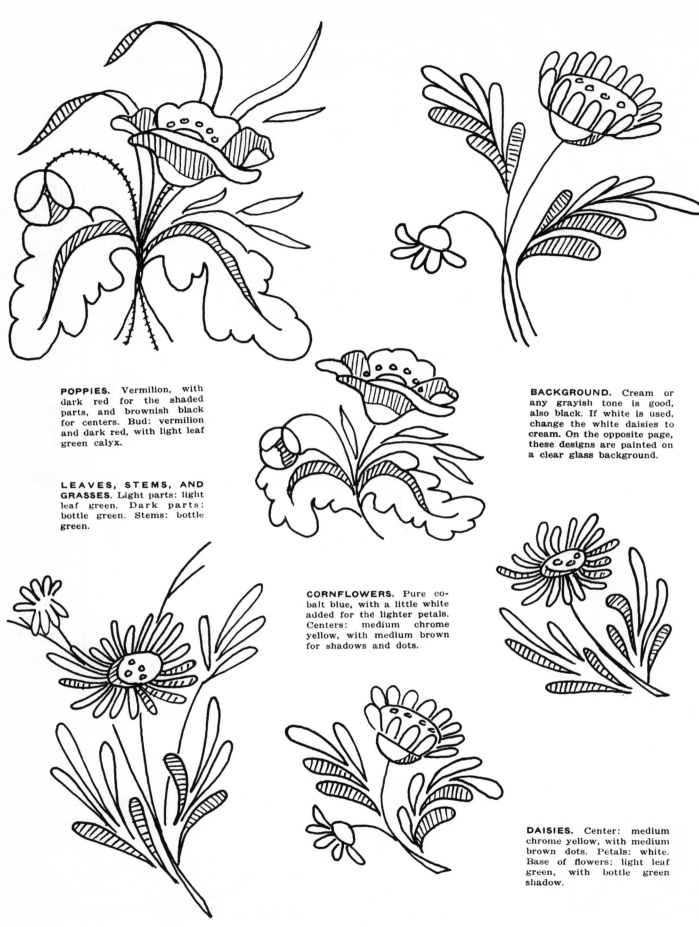

POPPIES. Vermilion, with dark red for the shaded parts, and brownish black for centers. Bud: vermilion and dark red, with light leaf green calyx.

LEAVES, STEMS, AND GRASSES. Light parts: light leaf green. Dark parts: bottle green. Stems: bottle green.

BACKGROUND. Cream or any grayish tone is good, also black. If white is used, change the white daisies to cream. On the opposite page, these designs are painted on a clear glass background.

CORNFLOWERS. Pure cobalt blue, with a little white added for the lighter petals. Centers: medium chrome yellow, with medium brown for shadows and dots.

DAISIES. Center: medium chrome yellow, with medium brown dots. Petals: white. Base of flowers: light leaf green, with bottle green shadow.

FIELD FLOWERS ON GLASS

When you have become convinced that tin cans may be turned into art treasures, your mind is sure to turn to bottles, old mayonnaise jars, and other articles of glass. Then you are on your way toward a kind of painting that has a distinctive charm. Bright designs on a transparent background are as fascinating as reflections in clear water. There is a sparkling quality about any piece of painted glass that gives it a special value no matter how lowly its origin.

Directions for painting on glass are given under Materials for Painting. Select bottles, jars, and other glass objects of interesting shape, and choose designs that will make a lacy pattern against the light. The field flowers used here are especially good. The smaller ones are painted on the underside of glass squares for coasters, the larger ones fit decanters and bottles for oil or vinegar. Painted jars and bottles for salt, soda, and lotions give any bathroom quite a lift. Dainty designs for covered glass jars are appropriate for baby gifts.

BACKGROUND. Part inside the frame: cream. Part outside the frame may be the same or a contrasting color such as gray green or lacquer red. This design is also effective on a natural wood background, or the part outside the frame may be black.

FRAME. Olive green with two cobalt blue flowers with chrome yellow centers.

WOMAN. Hair: black. Flesh: flesh color. Cheeks: dark coral. Lips: vermilion. Eyebrows and outline of nose: dark brown. Eyes: black. Neck bow: vermilion. Collar: white with cobalt blue scallops and dots. Cuffs to match collar. Front panel of dress: white with skirt trimming in cobalt, with pure cobalt for folds in skirt. Front lacing of bodice and sash: vermilion. Fan: coral pink, with ribs and design in cobalt.

MAN. Hat: cobalt blue with white feather. Wig: white with black bow. Flesh: flesh color. Cheek: dark coral. Mouth: vermilion. Eye: dark brown. Frills: white. Coat: vermilion with white outlining arm. Vest: lemon yellow. Buttons: lemon yellow. Trousers: cobalt blue. Stockings: white. Garters and shoes: black. Cane: black with lemon yellow head and tip. Rose in hand: vermilion with white outlining petals and dark leaf green for leaves, stem, and calyx.

[94]

MAN AND LADY. The lower part of this design is used for greeting cards only. Use a fine pointed brush in painting, and follow the colors outlined on the opposite page.

SHIP. Fill in light blue background around white sails, or paint the sails in white on blue. Rope ladders, rigging, and masts may be done with pen and ink. Body of ship: dark blue and golden tan. Shadows in water: dark blue. Flags and wind stocking: blue and red.

FLOWER DESIGN. Paint on a black, cream, or antiqued white ground. Center of flower: medium chrome yellow with orange dots around it. Shaded berries: wine red. Other large berries: cobalt blue. Small berries: orange. Stems and fine dots: medium brown. Leaves: bottle green with brown veins. Center petals of flower: pure cobalt blue. Outside petals: medium cobalt.

FOR GREETINGS AND BOXES

The romantic man and lady and the ship may be painted on small boxes or in water colors for hand-decorated greeting cards. The flower design is also good for boxes and small articles. The border may be increased in size or changed to fit objects of different shapes.

PAINT OUTDOOR FURNITURE

Ivy twining round your barbecue table will add to the romance of eating out of doors. You don't have to grow it, you can paint it, and if the winter blasts cause it to fade, all you have to do is touch it up in the spring. This design is particularly pleasing painted on a natural wood or a stained wood.

Lawn chairs and benches are generally not so rustic. Even the simplest types will take on quite an air if freshly painted white and then decorated in peasant flowers, strawberries, or bright blue morning-glories. Try this for a set on your terrace, and you will never wish for lovelier outdoor furniture. If the pieces are antiqued, add a final coat of spar varnish so that the finish will not rub off on clothing.

MORNING-GLORIES. Centers: white with orange pistil and brownish black dots. Outside of throat: pink lines on white ground. Shaded parts of flowers and buds: cobalt blue. Use light cobalt for parts not otherwise specified.

Use for trays, chair backs, and drawers. Part of motif may be omitted for long narrow spaces.

Repeat for border or long vine.

BACKGROUND. Cream, white, or black.

LEAVES AND STEMS. Leaves are light leaf green, with shaded parts bottle green. Use light leaf green for stems, calyx, and tendrils.

DUCK. May be painted white with feathers outlined in dark blue, or the body may be light chrome yellow with outlines of feathers in medium brown. Paint the eye white with dark brown center and outline around the edge. Bill and feet: burnt orange with dark brown shadow inside the bill.

CUT OUT AND PAINT A DUCK

It isn't what you do, but how you do it that counts. That is true of lawn ornaments. It is granted that most of them do not ornament, but here is proof that in a proper setting a really appealing duck cut out of a flat piece of wood can have a great deal of charm. He is at his best if painted snowy white against a background of deep green foliage and reflected in a pool be it ever so small.

In one yard the pool was only a shallow birdbath made by sinking an old tub in the ground, filling it partly full of small stones and gravel, then spreading on a two-inch layer of cement, and shaping it like a saucer. Flat stones were laid around the edge, and a small evergreen planted at one side. There the duck was placed, and whole families of robins came and waded in gingerly to the deepest part and

splashed and splashed until the forget-me-nots around the edge were soaked. The duck seemed perpetually pleased about it all.

And there was a small boy who was made happy by a pair of these ducks at the sides of a homemade wheelbarrow. He pushed them around all day and hauled prodigious loads of things that are of great consequence to a lad of five or six.

The ducks are quite easy to cut out of either plywood or solid material with a jig saw or even a hand coping saw. Plywood that is to be used out of doors must be the marine type made to withstand the weather. No amount of paint will keep the ordinary kind from warping and coming apart when wet. When painting the duck, color for eyes, feathers, beak and feet are put on after the body paint is dry.

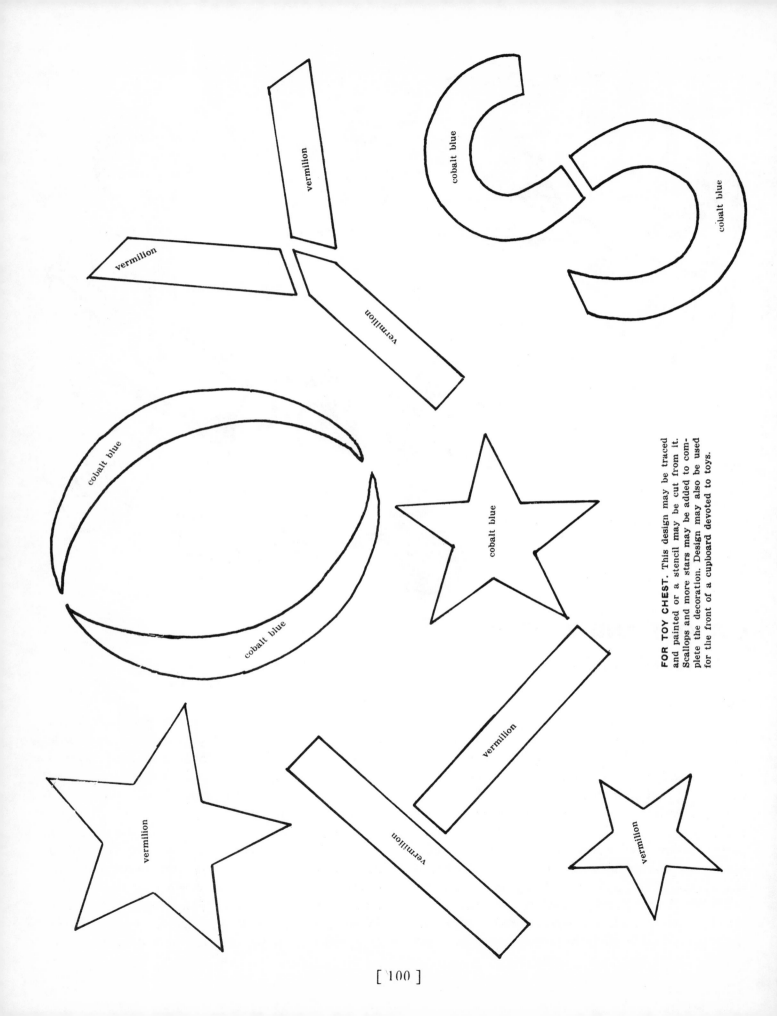

FOR TOY CHEST. This design may be traced and painted or a stencil may be cut from it. Scallops and more stars may be added to complete the decoration. Design may also be used for the front of a cupboard devoted to toys.

LAMP WITH PAINTED SHADE. This lamp base may be made from a set of toy blocks by drilling holes through them for the wiring and then gluing them together. Glue the center column first and let it dry under pressure. Also apply pressure while the glue for the side blocks is drying. If the glue is of good quality and is handled in this manner, the base will be almost as strong as if it were made in one piece. The marching children patterns, pages 110, 112, and 114, are used for the paper parchment shade.

STARS AND SCALLOPS FOR TOY CHEST AND TABLE. Red scallops and red and blue stars and letters on a white ground give this toy chest and table a circus-day air. The pieces are strictly homemade, enameled white before decorating. After decorations are dry, a number of coats of clear waterproof varnish may be applied to build up a hard washable finish. The painting patterns used may be found on pages 100 and 103.

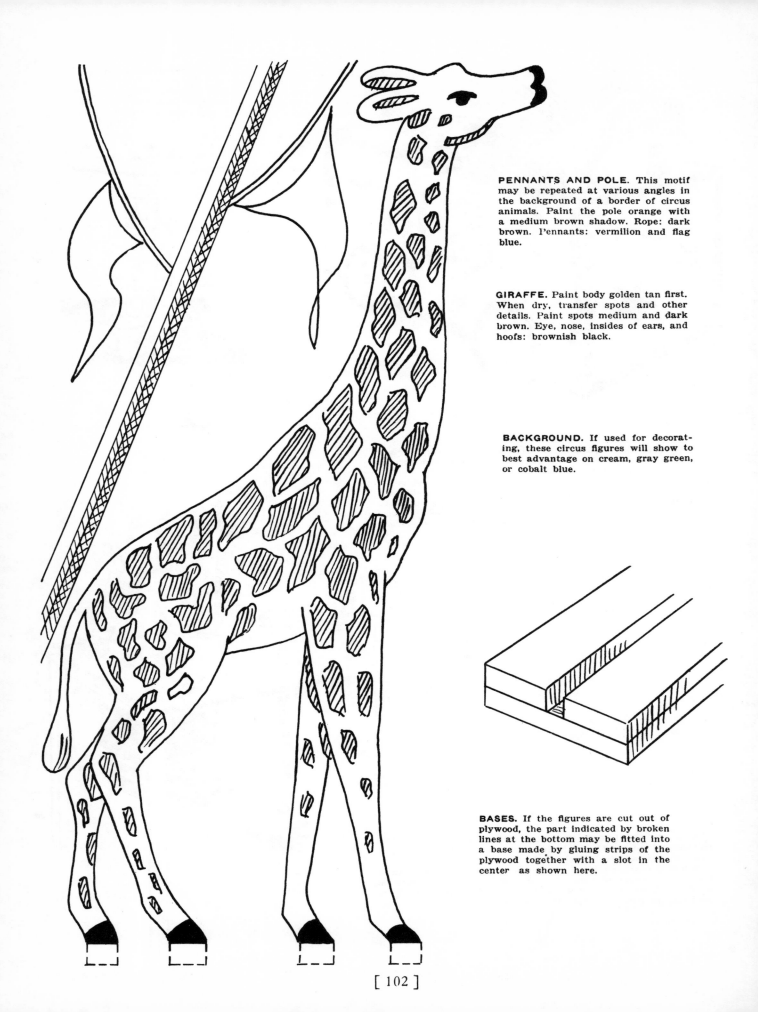

PENNANTS AND POLE. This motif may be repeated at various angles in the background of a border of circus animals. Paint the pole orange with a medium brown shadow. Rope: dark brown. Pennants: vermilion and flag blue.

GIRAFFE. Paint body golden tan first. When dry, transfer spots and other details. Paint spots medium and dark brown. Eye, nose, insides of ears, and hoofs: brownish black.

BACKGROUND. If used for decorating, these circus figures will show to best advantage on cream, gray green, or cobalt blue.

BASES. If the figures are cut out of plywood, the part indicated by broken lines at the bottom may be fitted into a base made by gluing strips of the plywood together with a slot in the center as shown here.

LION. Paint the entire body golden tan first. When dry, transfer details. Paint the medium shade indicated here, tan. Dark shadows: medium brown. Eye and nose: dark brown. Inside of mouth: vermilion.

Red and blue stars for nursery decorations.

Scallops for a wheel seven inches in diameter.

vermilion

cobalt blue

vermilion

Scallops for top of a play table.

vermilion

EVERY DAY IS CIRCUS DAY

Right this way to the Big Top that mother made to fit over a card table. Watch that young lion tamer do his stuff with the king of beasts! This circus, complete with a clown, is just one way that the patterns on the following pages may be used. Here the animals and clown are cut out of thin wood, fitted into wooden stands and painted in lifelike colors.

These figures also make beguiling wall decorations for a child's room. Or they may be painted on toy chests, play tables, beds, and other pieces of furniture. They combine well with all the other gay motifs given here for decorating nurseries and playrooms. The clown or the seal may be cut out of wood and painted to make lamp bases.

CLOWN. Paint entirely white and then transfer details to the white surface after it is dry. Paint pompons for hat and suit vermilion, also hat brim, nose, mouth, and ruffles. Shaded parts of ruffles: dark red. Hair, eye, and suit shadows: black. Cymbals: brassy yellow.

SEAL. Head, chest, and front of fin: tan. Body, eye, tip of nose, and whiskers: brownish black.

BOX. Top: light chrome yellow. Side: vermilion. Hand hold: brownish black.

BALL. Vermilion.

BASES. If the figures are cut out of plywood, the part indicated by broken lines at the bottom will fit into a base made as shown on page 102.

[105]

The dilapidated piece of furniture at the left was turned into a cupboard with one drawer. The other drawers were used to make storage chests. The furniture shown is cream color decorated in bright blues, greens, reds, and yellows. Circus animals and clown are used for wall decoration and lamp base. The glass articles on the cupboard are decorated in rosebuds and ribbon. Patterns used may be found on pages 51, 102, 103, 105, 107, 108, and 109.

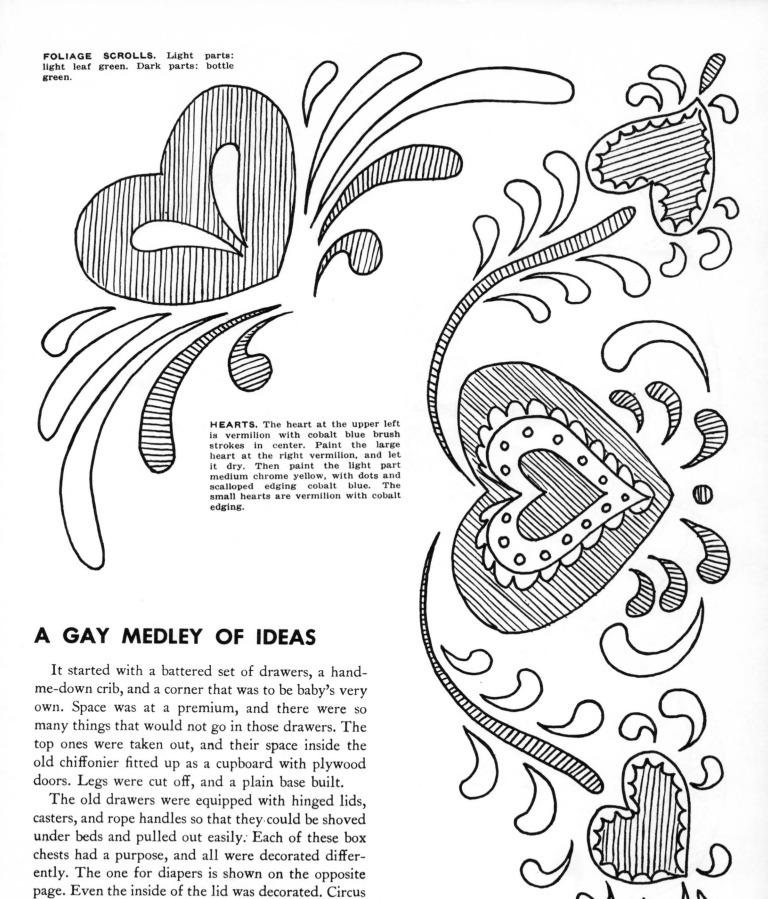

FOLIAGE SCROLLS. Light parts: light leaf green. Dark parts: bottle green.

HEARTS. The heart at the upper left is vermilion with cobalt blue brush strokes in center. Paint the large heart at the right vermilion, and let it dry. Then paint the light part medium chrome yellow, with dots and scalloped edging cobalt blue. The small hearts are vermilion with cobalt edging.

A GAY MEDLEY OF IDEAS

It started with a battered set of drawers, a hand-me-down crib, and a corner that was to be baby's very own. Space was at a premium, and there were so many things that would not go in those drawers. The top ones were taken out, and their space inside the old chiffonier fitted up as a cupboard with plywood doors. Legs were cut off, and a plain base built.

The old drawers were equipped with hinged lids, casters, and rope handles so that they could be shoved under beds and pulled out easily. Each of these box chests had a purpose, and all were decorated differently. The one for diapers is shown on the opposite page. Even the inside of the lid was decorated. Circus animals and clown, hearts, swags, and tassels are designs used in this corner in bright colors on a cream ground.

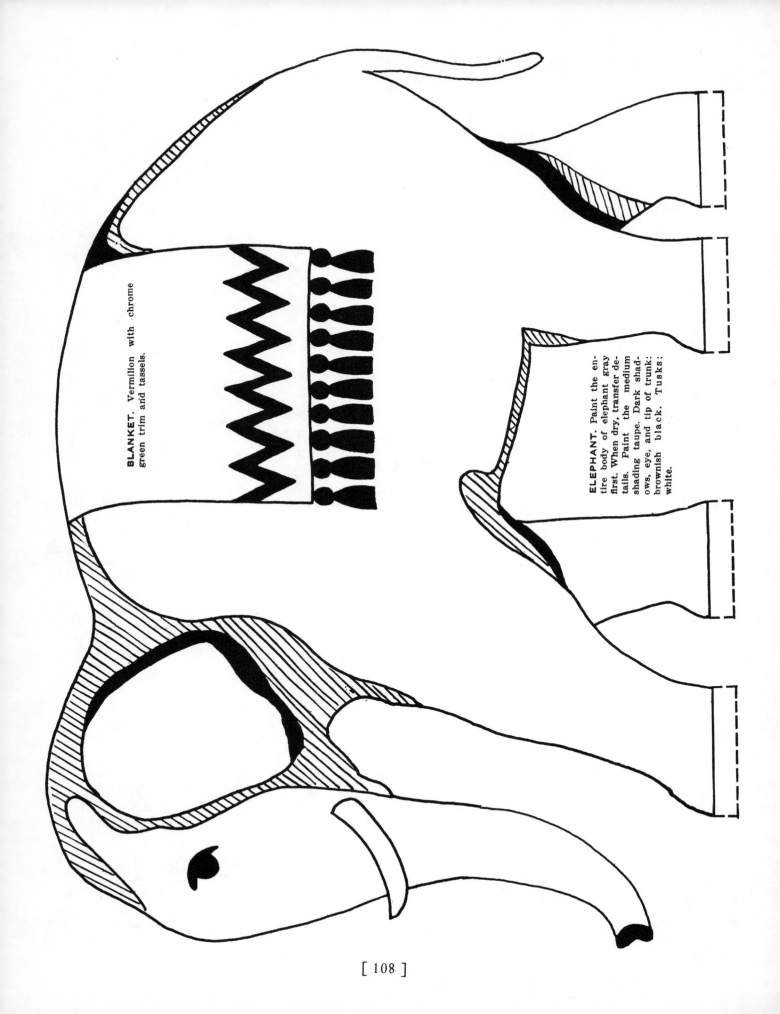

BLANKET. Vermilion with chrome green trim and tassels.

ELEPHANT. Paint the entire body of elephant gray first. When dry, transfer details. Paint the medium shading taupe. Dark shadows, eye, and tip of trunk: brownish black. Tusks: white.

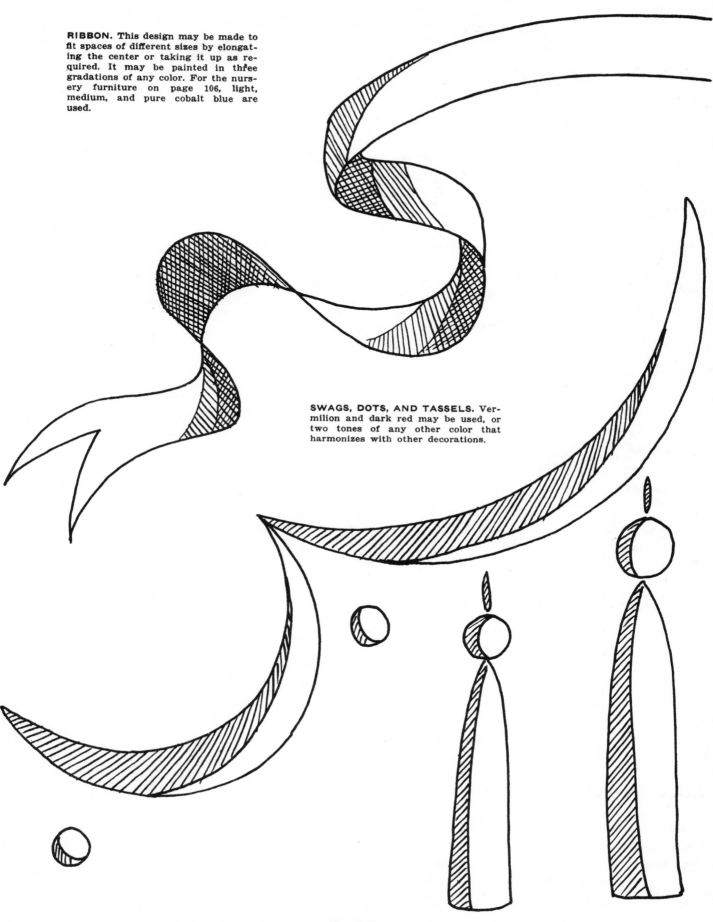

RIBBON. This design may be made to fit spaces of different sizes by elongating the center or taking it up as required. It may be painted in three gradations of any color. For the nursery furniture on page 106, light, medium, and pure cobalt blue are used.

SWAGS, DOTS, AND TASSELS. Vermilion and dark red may be used, or two tones of any other color that harmonizes with other decorations.

BACKGROUND. Cream or light gray slightly tinted with color. If a prepared cream color is not deep enough for white to show up well on it, add a little raw umber or chrome yellow.

HAIR. Light chrome yellow.

HAT. White.

FLESH. Sun tan, with dark coral for cheek.

DRUM. Top: white. Rims: brownish black. Sides: orange, with brownish black lines. Drumsticks: orange. Neck strap: orange.

APRON. Includes sash but not collar: light apple green.

DRESS. White, with apple green dots. Collar: white.

SOCKS. White.

SHOES. Brownish black.

FLOWER. White with chrome yellow center. Leaves: light leaf green.

GROUND LINES. Light leaf green.

Center of design.

MARCHING CHILDREN

There is nothing to painting these figures but tracing outlines and then filling in flat colors. The one important thing is to keep the edge of each painted area clean and sharp. If adjoining colors run together, paint separate parts, put the work aside until dry, and then paint adjoining parts. Flesh tones should be dry when eyes, noses, and mouths are painted. A little drier in your thinning liquid will speed this. The white hats and many colors show best on a cream or grayish ground.

LET'S START A PARADE

Marching children, bright bows, and quaint flowers are used here to turn odd pieces of furniture into a well-matched set that is as attractive as anything you might find for the room of a small boy or girl. The designs are full of life and action. A boy with a wooden sword and his Scottie dog. Another mounted on a broomstick horse. A third marches on with flag and horn, and a fourth breathlessly brings up the rear on his scooter. Girls beat drums and make a clatter with tin-pan cymbals.

Youngsters love this parade of marching children, and you will enjoy painting them. It is easy, and the figures seem to come to life as you fill in the flat colors indicated on the patterns. You may want to make a border on the wall, as well as use them for furniture. The bowknots and flowers are designed to fit drawer fronts, chair backs, and panels.

The furniture shown here was painted cream color first, then decorated, then rubbed with an antique overtone, and finally varnished with a number of coats of clear varnish to build up a very hard washable finish. The chair is of regular size with back and legs cut down and new knobs screwed into the tops of the back supports. These as well as all the drawer pulls match the red ribbons in the painted designs. The bedspread and seat cushion are red and white. A bright braided rag rug adds still more color.

SWORD AND HELMET. Gun-metal gray, with under brim of helmet brownish black.

FLESH. Sun tan, with dark coral for cheeks.

BACKGROUND. Same as for figure on page 110.

OVERALLS. Cobalt blue.

SHIRT. White.

DOG. Brownish black. Eye: medium brown. Nose: vermilion. Collar and leash: vermilion.

FLOWERS. Vermilion and cobalt blue. Leaves, stems, and ground lines: light leaf green.

SHOES AND SOCKS. Both figures: shoes brownish black; socks white.

FLAG. Vermilion, white, and flag blue. Stick and ball: orange.

HAT. White.

HAIR AND EYES. Boy with dog: chrome yellow hair and cobalt blue eyes. Boy with flag: brownish black hair and medium brown eyes.

TROUSERS. Cobalt blue, with flag blue shadow. White buttons.

SHIRT. Vermilion and white stripes.

HORN. Brassy yellow, with olive brown shadows.

dark red

vermilion

vermilion

vermilion

vermilion

vermilion

dark red

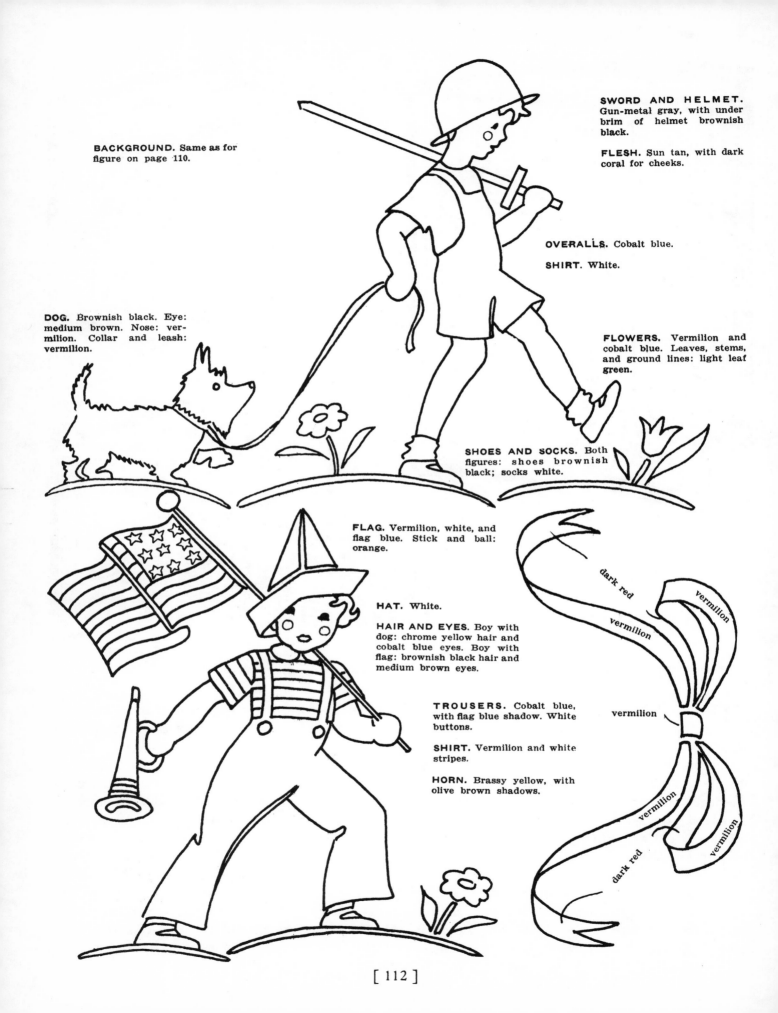

light cobalt

cobalt blue

cobalt blue

light cobalt

dark red

vermilion

vermilion

vermilion

dark red

vermilion

BACKGROUND. Deep cream.

FLOWER AT CENTER TOP. Two
top petals: vermilion. All other petals:
dark red. Center: medium chrome
yellow.

LEAVES AND STEMS. All bottle
green.

light cobalt

cobalt blue

vermilion

vermilion

dark red

vermilion

vermilion

dark red

light cobalt

cobalt blue

vermilion

vermilion

dark red

dark red

dark red

dark red

These flower and ribbon designs are used in combination with
figures of marching children for the furniture shown on page 111.
By repeating the designs, unmatched odds and ends of furniture
may be harmonized for a child's room.

BACKGROUND. Same as for figure on page 110.

HATS. All three, white. Orange feather for the boy on the horse.

FLESH. Sun tan, with dark coral for cheeks.

HAIR AND EYES. Boy on scooter: medium brown hair and cobalt blue eyes. Boy on horse: dark brown hair and eyes. Girl: brownish black hair, with rose ribbon; medium brown eyes.

SCOOTER. Handle, edges of board, edges and centers of wheels: brownish black. All the rest vermilion.

SWORD. Medium brown.

SUIT. Light cobalt blue, with inside of sleeves and other shadows pure cobalt. Collar, belt, and pocket: white.

SOCKS AND SHOES. All three have brownish black shoes and white socks.

FLOWERS. From left to right: cobalt blue, vermilion, white with chrome yellow center, vermilion, cobalt blue. Leaves, stems, and ground lines: light leaf green.

HORSE. Head: white. Mane, eye, nostril, and shadow inside ear: brownish black. Mouth and bridle: vermilion. Stick: orange.

DRESS. American Beauty rose. with white bands and sash.

CYMBALS. Brassy yellow, with olive brown shadows and handle.

SHIRT. White, with chrome yellow collar, cuffs, and front trimming.

TROUSERS. Chrome yellow, with medium brown belt.

[114]

STENCILED DECORATIONS

Old and new ways to cut and use stencil patterns

STENCILING generally is done by brushing paint through the cutout openings of a stencil pattern. The pattern must be stiff and firm so that the edges do not ruff up. A blunt round brush with short stiff bristles is used. Paint should be thinned just enough so that it will work easily but will not run under the stencil. It is applied with a dabbing motion. Stencil patterns may be used over and over, and they offer a quick method of reproducing repeats of the same design. The efficiency of the method is attested by the fact that in early American days whole walls were stenciled with repeat designs in imitation of wallpaper which was then very expensive.

The Hitchcock type of side chair, the Boston rocker, and many small stands and tables made in this country between 1826 and 1845 were stenciled to give the effect of hand-painted decoration. The stenciling was done by women, and old records show that chairs decorated in this way frequently sold for as little as a dollar or a dollar and a half. Yet despite the fact that the work was highly commercialized and done by a rather mechanical method, there is great charm in the decoration of these old pieces stenciled in gold or silver on black, or in color on soft green, yellow, or streaked brown ground.

Stenciling with gold and other metal powders became an art in itself with so much distinction and individuality that the old methods are well worth our study. Trays, boxes, and other small articles of tin as well as chairs were stenciled in gilt, silver, bronze, and some colored metallic powders applied to give shaded effects of great depth and beauty. Designs of grape leaves, fruit, melons, urns, and flowers are typical of the period. Several of these old designs have been reproduced here in stencil patterns that may be cut out and used in one piece.

If you should be lucky enough to find an old chair or tray that shows the original design dimly, try to copy the design and cut a stencil to use to restore the piece. If the design seems complicated, remember that the stenciled parts frequently were retouched with freehand flourishes. Also, overlapped effects were obtained by using different stencils for different parts. With a little study the stenciled outlines of each part will become clear.

Cutting stencil patterns. Architects' linen is good to use for cutting the stencil pattern for one of these complicated designs to be done in gold powder, as it is stiff and firm and yet may be cut with manicure scissors. Simple designs to be done in color are usually cut in heavy paper that has been shellacked. The design is traced on the stiffened paper, which is placed over a piece of glass and cut out with a razor blade or a sharp knife. There are two different ways to prepare color stencils. One is to cut a different stencil for each color and each shade or variation of the color. The other is to use a design that has been simplified in such a way that bridges of the stencil paper are left between all colors. This type of design may be cut in one piece, and different colors stenciled in different openings. A number of these simplified designs are given here.

Stenciling with metallic powder. And so we have the stiff linen stencil to be used with gold or other metal powder and the two types of stencil patterns to be used for color. The shaded effect of the gold powder stenciling is obtained by rubbing powder on a varnished surface that is not quite dry. The first step is to paint the piece with flat black paint. When this is dry, rub varnish on the part that is to be stenciled, using a soft cloth or your bare hand. Allow this to dry two or three hours or until it is sticky but does not rub off. Place the stencil pattern over this sticky surface. The varnish will hold it in place.

Place a piece of velvet or chamois over your forefinger and dip it in the metallic powder, taking up as little as possible. Rub this into the stencil opening, shading it by means of light or heavy pressure. Keep the edges sharp by rubbing away from the edges and toward the center of the stencil openings. The parts where the least gold is used and the black shows through the most will be the dark or shadow side of each part of each motif. Think of the light coming from one direction throughout the design. Most of the old designs give the effect of light from the upper left throwing shadows toward the right.

When the stenciling is finished, pick up every bit of loose dust before removing the pattern. Striping and outlining for seats, backs, and spindles of chairs, and the edges of trays was done freehand in the old days with a fine brush in lemon yellow paint instead of in gold because gold paint does not flow evenly. These narrow lines of color add an interesting accent. If your hand is not steady enough to do this striping, use masking tape at each side of the outline and remove it when the paint is dry. After the stenciling and striping is done, apply several coats of clear varnish to the whole piece. When the varnish is dry, the high gloss may be rubbed down with powdered pumice if desired.

A stencil for each color. When a separate stencil is used for each color and for the different variations of one color, it is possible to get a feeling of depth in the design by stenciling first the lightest part of each motif and then, when the paint is dry, stenciling the shadows. Overlapped effects also may be obtained in this way, and it is possible to reproduce almost any design in a slightly simplified form by cutting a number of stencils. Of course each part of the design must register or fit together perfectly. This is done by making all the pattern pieces exactly the same size and then marking the outside edge of the first one with chalk on the object that is being stenciled. The edges of all the other stencil pattern pieces are then placed to fit these register marks. Scotch tape is good to hold the stencil pattern in place. A fairly large stencil brush may be used when one color is being applied at a time. Be sure that each color is perfectly dry before the next stencil is applied.

One stencil for all colors. When one stencil with bridges is cut for a whole design, different colors may be stenciled through different openings. This is a very quick process as no time is lost in waiting for each color to dry before another is stenciled. As in all stenciling, the pattern should be anchored firmly. The paint should be applied with a quick dabbing motion—never with strokes toward the edges of the openings as this will cause the color to run under the stencil pattern. A stencil brush not more than a quarter of an inch in diameter should be used so that small spaces may be stenciled without running over into an opening to be stenciled in another color.

All the colors stenciled in this manner are flat with no illusion of depth or shading. This is especially good for Dutch designs which were generally painted in flat color. After the stencil has been removed, some of the spaces left by the bridges in the pattern may be filled in by hand to give a more natural effect if desired. Shading and other details also may be added if you wish to give the design a freer, less conventional appearance. If you are painting a number of cupboard doors alike or gifts or small articles to sell, much time may be saved by stenciling the main part of the design and then adding freehand touches to give a hand-painted appearance. This is a short cut for which there is precedent in many highly prized antiques.

GOLD STENCILING ON BLACK

In the early eighteen hundreds many side chairs and rockers as well as trays, tea caddies, and other articles of tin were decorated in beautifully shaded stencil designs in gold on a black ground. It is always a satisfaction to restore a piece of this sort to its original condition if the design has grown dim. New pieces of tinware also may be decorated in the fine old designs used so long ago.

One of these old stencil patterns is reproduced here at the left, and the method of rubbing gold powder through the openings of a cutout stencil onto a surface covered with slightly sticky varnish is illustrated here. Velvet or chamois is used over the forefinger, which is dipped in the powder, and the rubbing is done with varying pressure to produce the shading.

This process and the method of preparing the work are more fully described in the text on stenciled decorations. Several other gold stencil designs are also given here. Collecting such designs by tracing them from old pieces is an interesting hobby, and the work of restoring or reproducing gold stenciling by this original method is indeed rewarding.

GOLD POWDER

SCROLLS FOR BACK OF ROCKER. The broken lines indicate the shape of the back of a Boston rocker and show how this scroll motif joins the flower designs on pages 66 or 119 in decorating such a chair. The long narrow motif may be used along the fronts of chair seats or for the backs of side chairs.

Small scroll motifs may be combined or used separately for borders or fillers around edges of trays with flowers in the center.

COLORS. These scrolls are usually painted in light lemon yellow on a cream or black ground. Start to paint each scroll at the widest part, and taper it by easing the pressure on the brush.

where strokes overlap, a slightly shaded effect results. This shading may be accented by retouching with deeper lemon yellow or with olive green.

[118]

Designs to be stenciled in gold on black.

IF YOU USE STENCILS

Two small chests of drawers, a long mirror, and a handmade stool are made into a vanity unit with the help of the stencil shown at the left. These designs, especially planned for stenciling, are cut out and different colors stenciled through openings with the small blunt stencil brush.

The canisters below are stenciled by cutting a different stencil for each color. A larger stencil brush then may be used, but each color must be allowed to dry before the next is applied, and care must be used so that the register of colors is perfect.

Below at the left is a Hitchcock chair stenciled in gold by the method explained here. At the right below is a design for a stenciled scroll with shadows to be added by hand after the stenciling is done.

COFFEE SUGAR FLOUR

RICE OAT MEAL RAISINS TEA

STENCIL OR TRACING DESIGN. This pattern will hold together in one piece if it is used for cutting a stencil, or it may be traced and painted in the usual way.

BACKGROUND. Cream, white, black, or any grayish tone.

BIRD. Head: vermilion. Body outlines and feathers: cobalt blue. Wing: bottle green. Tail: vermilion. Beak and feet: medium chrome yellow. Branch and leaves: bottle green.

HEART AND FLOWERS. Heart: vermilion. Leaves and stems: bottle green. Flowers: cobalt blue with medium chrome yellow centers, and small bottle green leaves at sides.

TULIPS. Leaves and stems: bottle green. Outside petals of tulips: vermilion. Center petal: medium chrome yellow. Small petals: cobalt blue.

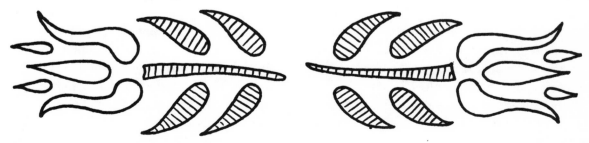

[121]

COLOR FOR A MODERN KITCHEN

Cleanliness, convenience, and plenty of cupboards are the watchwords for a modern kitchen, but they should not add up to a room that lacks the cozy comfort of the old-time kitchen or one that goes overboard on the side of quaintness by camouflaging an up-to-date stove or sink.

Many ideas from other times and periods fit logically into the modern scheme of things. In gay and colorful Dutch kitchens, cupboard doors were usually treated as decorative panels. All sorts of useful articles were decorated in a manner that harmonized with other things in the room. The stove or the fireplace where meals were cooked was almost always the center of interest in old kitchens.

Some of these ideas are shown here in a modern setting. The designs for cupboard doors and drawers were inspired by old Pennsylvania Dutch designs. The wooden racks for the electric clock, spices, and

stainless steel knives are patterned after Early American models. They are decorated with little borders and hex designs, and who knows but what the hexes may keep away evil spirits just as they were supposed to do in an earlier day?

In decorating this kitchen, stencils were cut for the repeat designs for the lower cupboard doors, the drawers, and the borders on the stove side of the room. The bird designs for the upper cupboards were traced and then painted in a freer manner. This method also was used for the wooden racks and for the cooky container on the open shelf, which is a large bread pan with a wooden lid. Soft powder blue is the background color throughout. Counter tops are darker blue, floor terra-cotta red. Stove handles and other accents are brighter red. The painting patterns used may be found on pages 40, 41, and 123.

Repeat colors for parts that are alike.

dark red   dark red

vermilion

light leaf green

vermilion

dark red

vermilion

dark red   dark red

dark red

vermilion

vermilion

vermilion

dark red

dark red

vermilion

LONG DESIGN IN FOUR PARTS. Sections may be joined as indicated by the broken lines and arrows.

light leaf green   bottle green

light leaf green

light leaf green

light leaf green

STENCIL OR TRACE. These motifs are designed in such a way that a stencil may be cut from them if desired.

chrome yellow

light leaf green

cobalt blue

chrome yellow

light leaf green

vermilion

light leaf green

vermilion

FOR DRAWERS.

[123]

ABCDEFGHIJKLMNO
PQRSTUJVWXYZ
abcdefghijklmnopqr
stuvwxyz   23456789

ABCDEFGHI

JKLMNOPQ

RSTUVWXYZ

abcdefghijklmn   123455

opqrstuvwxyzz   367890

ABCDEFGHIJ
KLMNOPQRS
TUVWXYZ

abcdefghijklmn
opqrstuvwxyz;

IF YOU USE LETTERING

If you want to letter a word on a can, a box, or a bottle to indicate the contents, simple letters, such as are shown at the top of the opposite page, are effective and easy to paint. If you want to do a motto or other inscription, you might paint it in your own handwriting or a more formal script, such as is shown here. Any script will stand out more artistically if extra shading is added to all down strokes.

If you are really pretty good at lettering, you might use the Old English letters shown above. They are especially strong for anything that you want to individualize with initials. Script initials are more feminine. If your hand is not steady in making fine lines with a brush, you can letter on any dull-painted surface with india ink and a lettering pen.

Unless you have a good deal of practice, you will find it best to block in the letters on paper to fill the required space and then trace them onto the object to be decorated. If you would avoid amateurish work, do not allot the same amount of space to each letter. Some letters are narrow, as F, I, and J. Some are wide, as M and W. Some are roundish, as C, G, and O. Others are irregular, as L and T. Space the letters to give an even tone without too much light background showing at any one point. Allow less space for narrow letters. Do not crowd wide letters or they will look too dark. Let roundish letters and irregular ones cut into the light space around other letters wherever this will help to keep the general tone even.

BORDERS WITH MANY USES

If you paint many trays, boxes, lamp shades, and other small articles, you will find that you need a variety of little borders and fillers. Some skilled workers mark off the spacing for the design first, others judge the spacing by eye and paint brush-stroke borders and ray designs as quickly and easily as scribbling a word. If you feel more confidence with an outline to guide you, think of it as a guide only. Practice filling the spaces with a single stroke of the brush, bearing down or easing the pressure to obtain the effect you want. Soon you will be working as freely as anyone.

Some of these borders are painted in one tone only. Others are retouched with a darker shade to give the effect of a shadow. Still others are done in two or three contrasting colors, repeating the colors in a definite color scheme. An effect of a gold border is often obtained by painting little borders in two tones of lemon yellow. Ray designs also are painted in yellow, or they may repeat the colors of leaves or flowers. Leaf borders are always effective, and a combination of leaves and berries gives opportunity to repeat other colors in a design.

TRAY DESIGN. This border is an Early American design which may be expanded to fit larger trays by adding repeats of flower and leaf motifs along sides or ends as needed. The corner motifs will remain the same for trays of all sizes. The border may be used separately with good effect in decorating boxes and other articles.

BACKGROUND. The tray or other article to be decorated is enameled black first. When this is dry, the background for the flower and leaf part of the design is painted white. When the white is dry, the design is transferred.

BORDER. The bands at the sides of the border are painted medium chrome yellow. Large leaves: light leaf green with bottle green brush strokes in center. Stems and small leaves: bottle green. Outside part of flower petals: vermilion. Inside part of each petal: bottle green. Center of flower: medium chrome yellow. Inner border of small scrolls: medium chrome yellow.

CORNER MOTIFS. Light parts of shell: vermilion. Shaded parts: bottle green. Dot: medium chrome yellow, with shaded part bottle green.

More
Painting Patterns
for Home Decorators
Book 2

More Painting Patterns

for Home Decorators
Book 2

by

RUTH WYETH SPEARS

CONTENTS

Basic Supplies Obtainable at Local Art Supply Shops

Materials for painting designs on wood, tin, glass and pottery

Artists' tube oil colors: American vermilion, medium chrome yellow, cobalt blue, medium chrome green, zinc white; others, if desired.

Red sable watercolor brushes:
  1 brush ¼ inch diameter at base of ferrule
  1 brush ⅛ inch
Flat bristle brush 1 inch wide for backgrounds
  of small articles
2- to 3-ounce container clear white waterproof
  varnish

2- to 3-ounce container japan drier
3 ounces turpentine
Palette and palette knife (optional)
Mat-finish or high-gloss enamel for back-
  grounds
Tube raw Turkey umber for antique finishes

Materials for painting and stenciling on fabric

Colorfast textile paint. Start with ¾-ounce jars. A wide range of colors may be mixed with red, yellow, blue, black and white.

Several ¾-ounce jars extendor
2- to 3-ounce container special thinner for use
  with fabric paint
2- to 3-ounce container special brush cleaner for
  use with fabric paint
Round stencil brush ¼ inch diameter with stiff
  bristles

Fine-pointed hair or bristle brush
Speed-ball pen
Translucent stencil paper
Stencil knife
White blotting paper
Thumbtacks
Scotch masking tape

Materials for painting greeting cards

Two-ply kid-finish Bristol board
Single-ply drawing paper for use with ink or
  watercolor
Transparent watercolors. A wide range of colors
  may be mixed from spectrum red, yellow
  and blue.

Opaque white watercolor
Opaque cobalt blue watercolor
Red sable watercolor brushes sizes 0 and 2
Waterproof black India ink
Fine sketching pen
Speed-ball pen

ACTUAL-SIZE TRACING PATTERNS

FOREWORD

An exciting, absorbing hobby was discovered by many people when they bought a copy of PAINTING PATTERNS FOR HOME DECORATORS, Book 1. Some of them had never held a brush before. They were thrilled to get immediate results by using tracing patterns and color guides and by following illustrated steps for everything from brush-stroke painting to gold stenciling.

It seemed in the beginning that this first book contained enough actual-size tracing designs to keep painting enthusiasts happy indefinitely. But soon there were requests for more painting patterns. More designs to decorate trays, gifts and bridge prizes were in demand. Crafts teachers wanted more patterns for students to use. Homemakers were interested in designs to freshen up old furnishings and to add cheer to bleak but efficient kitchens. More designs for hand-painted greeting cards were requested.

More Painting Patterns. The idea began to take shape. It seemed clear that this new set of patterns should supplement PAINTING PATTERNS FOR HOME DECORATORS, Book 1, which contained many basic designs and directions. Also, since the publication of the first book, new washable fabric paints had become generally available. It was decided that complete directions for this type of painting would give hobbyists a fascinating new field for the application of designs.

Work on MORE PAINTING PATTERNS FOR HOME DECORATORS, Book 2, began in earnest. Museums, libraries and private sources were searched for regional and period motifs. Old-fashioned flowers in the author's garden also were a de-sign source. In the heat of summer, when inspiration was needed for Christmas cards, a sprig of holly was picked from a neighbor's bush.

Many experiments were made with fabric painting. The kind of paint and method are outlined here. The kinds of watercolors and ink to use for hand-decorated greeting cards also are fully treated. The paints to use for all the other projects in this book are the same five basic oil paints used in Book 1. They are American vermilion, medium chrome yellow, cobalt blue, medium chrome green, and zinc white. Every variation of these colors mentioned in this book may be mixed by following one of the more than sixty mixing formulas in Book 1. Turpentine with a little clear varnish in it is a good mixing medium.

The chapters in Book 1 on preparing surfaces and on glazes and overtones contain essential information, and the chapter on transferring designs offers many helpful suggestions. Here, in Book 2, I should like to stress again how useful a pad of architects' transparent tracing paper is when you are preparing to apply one of the designs in either book. Place a sheet of it over the pattern and trace the outlines with a sharp pencil. This gives you a duplicate pattern which is easy to work with and may be turned over to make facing designs. The paper is treated so that pencil lines on the under side may be transferred by tracing over the outlines from the upper side without using carbon paper. Also, it is easy to make slight adaptations on this transparent pattern which may be needed to make it fit the object to be decorated.

COLORS FOR FRAME. The coloring for leaves, stems and scrolls of design on title page is light leaf and bottle green. Flowers similar to those on this page follow coloring outlined here. The smaller flowers are yellow and orange. The berries are orange. A tracing pattern for a smaller border using these motifs is given on the opposite page and is shown in color on Page 25.

FLOWERS. Light flowers, all medium cobalt blue. Flowers at top, dotted areas, medium chrome yellow. Petals shaded with straight lines, orange. Dots at base of these flower petals are orange.

BIRDS. Lightest parts, cobalt blue. Parts shaded with straight lines, medium chrome green. Parts shaded with crossed lines, bottle green. Dotted areas, yellow. Eyes, white and brownish black.

BACKGROUND. Either black or cream color may be used with good effect for this design. A rather dark antique glaze should be used as a final finish for a tray with a light background. Rub the glaze on to give a slightly mottled effect as suggested in directions in Book 1.

HAND-PAINTED TRAYS AND TINWARE

If you want to paint something of outstanding value, a handsome tray probably will be your first choice. A beautiful tray does double duty. It holds its own as decoration in any home while at the same time it stands ready for utilitarian service. Also worth your consideration is the fact that if you decide to paint a tray there is a fair chance that your handiwork may become an antique of tomorrow.

From early Georgian times, through the Victorian period, and right down to the present day, painted trays have had places of honor in well-furnished homes. A tray plus a folding stand makes a tea or coffee table of real distinction. A large tray standing on edge on a serving table or sideboard fills an important wall space and lends as much interest as a mirror or picture.

If you paint your tray carefully and apply a good waterproof finish it undoubtedly will play some such important role and be handed down to be enjoyed by future generations. Your choice of design should be of enduring quality too. A good tray design should have character. Its lasting charm depends upon rhythm of line and balance in the repetition of color, not just pretty naturalistic painting.

The shape of the tray is important. It is possible now to buy blank reproductions of many old-fashioned types. However, in most households there are old tin trays that need redecorating. Inexpensive oval, round and rectangular serving trays, such as may be purchased in any department store, also may be enameled any desired color and then decorated, or the original enamel may serve as background.

Small trays have become indispensable to modern living. A set of tiny trays to hold an individual glass and a canapé is useful. Round, painted tin lap trays are wonderful for buffet suppers. They are really painted pie tins. Large, rectangular cooky tins also make good serve-yourself trays for parties. One of these will hold everything for an individual dinner or luncheon.

As with trays, so with other pieces of decorated tinware. They never go out of style, and they seem particularly right in today's homes which depend so much upon effects gained with colorful accents against a simple background. A brightly painted cigarette or trinket box, a lamp base made of a canister, a painted tin wastebasket, desk accessories, wall pockets for plants, and dozens of other things of painted tin are popular and expensive items in gift shops. You can paint them yourself for almost nothing.

There are a few special tricks about painting on tin. They are fully explained in Book 1. Give special heed to the caution about removing all traces of oily film, wax, soap or grease of any sort from the tin surface before applying paint. Read well the directions about base coats of rust-inhibitive paint such as red lead. Take to heart the instructions for successive rubbings of coats of background enamel with very fine sandpaper. And finally, if you would have a piece of painted tin that really glows with soft rich color, follow one of the formulas for glazes and antique finishes.

TRAY DESIGN ON OPPOSITE PAGE. This Pennsylvania Dutch bird design may be used for a large tray by combining it with the flower and scroll design that frames the title page of this book. For a smaller tray, the border given on this page may be used. Colors for framing borders are outlined on the opposite page. These bird and flower motifs were adapted from a fragment of elaborately illustrated Fractur writing now in the Philadelphia Museum of Art. The work was probably a part of a birth certificate lettered and decorated by Heinrich Otto in the latter part of the eighteenth century.

OTHER TRAY DESIGNS. There are seventeen pages of tray patterns and ways to use them in this book. One group is on the following pages and another starts on Page 56. Many of the smaller designs given here for boxes and other articles also are suitable for small trays. It also follows that designs planned especially for trays may have other uses. Any of the large designs would be good for painting a window shade or a wastebasket or a cupboard door. Many of the tray border motifs may be adapted for decorating drawer fronts and chair backs, boxes or lamp shades.

EARLY AMERICAN TRAY DESIGN. The art of painting brush-stroke flower and leaf designs reached a high degree of refinement in this country in the early nineteenth century, and many people still own greatly prized trays of that period. The design on the opposite page and the border motifs on this page are taken from such a tray. Application of the design, and the coloring are shown on Pages 44 and 45.

BACKGROUND. A black background is traditional for a tray of this sort. A glaze of clear waterproof varnish rubbed with oil and pumice after the painting is dry will give the colors depth and richness and add the desired old-look.

HOW TO PAINT THE ROSES. The rose in color on Page 45 has been painted to show how the brush strokes are placed. All blending was avoided so that this would be clear. Even without any blending, the design is effective. The actual method of painting, however, is to paint the whole rose the middle tone of rosy pink and then, while this is still wet, paint in the dark brush strokes of American vermilion and the highlights of white. The pressure of the brush blends the wet colors just enough to give a slightly softer effect than is shown here, yet each brush stroke should be distinct with the sweep of the strokes from the outside petals toward the center of the rose. The buds are painted white first with three red strokes added while the white is wet.

LEAVES AND STEMS. The stems and the shaded leaves are bottle green. The light leaves are light leaf green. If you do not have a steady hand, a speed-ball pen purchased in an art supply store may be used instead of a brush for fine stems and yellow veins in large leaves.

DOTS. The lemon yellow dots placed here and there through the design are an old device used to add color balance.

This graceful tray design is an adaptation of tropical bird and flower motifs found in lacquer painting from the State of Michoacan Mexico. Other uses and adaptations are shown on Pages 14 and 15. Parts of the design, which may be painted on either a black or a lighted ground, are shown in color on Page 17.

TROPICAL FLOWERS AND BIRDS

In the city of Mexico at the National Museum of Fine Arts there is a collection of native crafts which is a rich source of inspiration for any designer. The variety of designs is bewildering. Some show great refinement. Others are startlingly similar to designs used in the folk arts of Europe. Here and there a design has a distinct Oriental style. The reason for this diversity is clear enough. Mexico is a country of villages where ancient crafts persist, yet it has for its capitol one of the most cosmopolitan cities in the world.

The charming pair of birds and tropical flower motifs in this design were found among examples of lacquer work from the State of Michoacan. The original design in its entirety was extremely involved. It was necessary to weave the motifs into a new design suitable for painting on trays and a wide variety of other objects. Matching borders and extra motifs were designed to be added where needed. The success of the experiment is clearly shown by the applications illustrated. The designs are adaptable and especially appropriate for tinware of all types.

This design of bright tropical birds painted on a black ground
seems especially appropriate for an old-fashioned octagonal tray.
The leaf border in gold may be painted or stenciled in green.

A large cooky tin makes a tray of useful size. When preparing it
for decorating be sure to use a priming coat of red lead or of
varnish before applying the background color.

WAYS TO USE DESIGNS. Patterns for the repeats for the flower-spray border of the tropical bird and flower design are given in two sizes, so that they may be used to decorate both large and small trays as well as such things as the tin box shown on this page. These sprays are designed so that four of them form a circle, or they may be used to make a straight border. Single sprays also have decorative possibilities or one of a pair may be reversed to face in the opposite direction. The latter arrangement is especially good for decorating drawer fronts for a chest of drawers that has been enameled glossy black. The slight changes in the bird design shown on these two pages also make it useful for a wide variety of things. The tracing patterns for these motifs are on Pages 13 and 16. The methods used for preparing both tin and wood for decorating are treated in detail in Book 1.

ABOVE. A big old canister of the type that was once used for imported tea and spices makes a good lamp base to paint. Lacking one of these, try to find in your local hardware store or in a mail order catalogue, a milk can or pail of the right size and shape. A bail or a lid handle may be removed.

LEFT. A tin candy box becomes a real work of art when decorated. It is fun to collect metal boxes of all sizes to paint. Typewriter ribbon boxes and tobacco tins make attractive painted stamp and trinket boxes.

[15]

This tracing pattern is given in two sizes, so that the design may be used for large and small objects.

BACKGROUND. These motifs are most striking when painted on a black ground. White or a soft greenish gray also give a good effect.

COLOR GUIDE FOR MOTIFS ON OPPOSITE PAGE. The colors used for painting the tropical bird and flower designs are, medium chrome yellow, burnt orange. medium cobalt blue, light leaf green, bottle green, and American vermilion. The burnt orange is a mixture of the yellow and vermilion red. The blue is pure cobalt with a little white. The light leaf green is medium chrome green lightened with yellow. The bottle green is medium chrome green darkened with cobalt and vermilion.

HOW TO USE FABRIC PAINTS

For stenciling and
for freehand painting

IN ITS modern version, painting on fabric is not at all the same thing as when our great grandmothers painted roses and forget-me-nots on velvet cushions. Today, things made of hand-painted materials are sold with the assurance that they may be laundered or dry-cleaned. Special textile paints made by new chemical processes make this possible.

The kind of paint. There are a number of kinds of textile paints. They may be purchased at stores that handle art supplies. Be sure that they have a colorfast guaranty and ask for special directions required for using them. The most common type of textile paint comes in small glass jars in a good range of basic colors which may be mixed to make a wide variety of hues and shades. A white substance called an extendor is mixed with these paints to add bulk and give the colors permanency. A special penetrating thinner and a jar of special brush cleaner also are essential though they are not always included in beginners' kits. The thinner should be used sparingly. However, the natural consistency of the paint is quite thick and it hardens quickly in the mixing dish and on brushes unless a little thinner is used as a mixing medium.

Brushes. A round stencil brush with stiff bristles such as is shown on the opposite page is needed. When doing free brushwork without a stencil most workers like medium-size and fine bristle brushes rather than soft hair brushes though either may be used successfully if the paint mixture is the right consistency. A fine pointed brush is needed for adding details to stenciled work. A speed-ball pen also is often used for outlining. If you do much fabric painting, you will want a number of brushes so that you will not have to clean one each time that you change colors.

Stencil paper and knife. Stencils are cut in stiff paper that has been treated so that it does not absorb the paint. A translucent kind with a paraffinlike surface is available at most stores where textile paints are sold. This type of stencil paper is easy to cut and is especially good to use in connection with this book

as the printed designs show through it and may be traced in preparation for cutting (see Steps 1 and 2 opposite page). A stencil knife of the type shown in Step 2 is best to use.

Other materials required. Small mixing dishes will be needed. Some workers use the glass tops of fruit jars. White blotting paper and thumb tacks are necessary, and a small roll of Scotch drafting tape is good to have to use for masking tape and to hold work in place. As with all painting, a good supply of clean, soft rags should be at hand.

Preparing the fabric for painting. White and light colored cottons, rayons, silks, linens and woolens are best for painting. Fabric should be washed with soap and warm water to remove starch or sizing. Press and then place white blotting paper under the part to be decorated and stretch it over a board. Hold it in place with thumb tacks or Scotch tape.

Method of working with textile paints. For a beginner, stenciling is easier to do with textile colors than free painting with a traced outline for a guide. Stenciling also has the advantage of being quicker when a design is to be repeated a number of times as it is so often in painting fabrics. A free effect may be obtained in stenciling by adding details later with a brush or a speed-ball pen. Most of the stencil patterns in this book call for these free touches. Shading added while you are stenciling also helps to give a more natural effect. After you have stenciled a few articles according to the directions on the opposite page, you will have the feel of working with this medium and will be ready to paint on fabric without a stencil. The trick is in learning to use just the right amount of the thinner so that the paint will work smoothly and at the same time will neither run nor build up in a thick mass. The colors are easy to mix and a good range of shaded tints may be made by combining them.

Setting the colors. Allow paint to dry twenty-four hours and then place a dry cloth over the design and press slowly with a warm iron. Press in the same manner from the other side. Then repeat several times.

STENCILING WITH FABRIC PAINT

LEFT, THE PATTERN. This is a tracing pattern for a daisylike flower with yellow petals, an orange and red center, and green leaves and stem. The steps below show how stencils are cut for the yellow and green portions of the design and how they are stenciled on the fabric.

RIGHT, THE FINISHING TOUCHES. This sketch shows the center of the flower being painted with free brush strokes after the petals, stem and leaves have been stenciled. It would be possible to stencil the center by cutting separate stencils for the orange and the red. However, finishing touches added with a free brush give a stenciled design a softer less mechanical appearance.

stencil paper over pattern

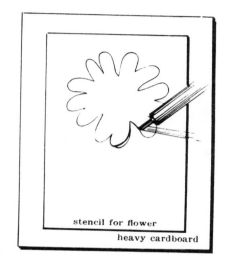

stencil for flower

heavy cardboard

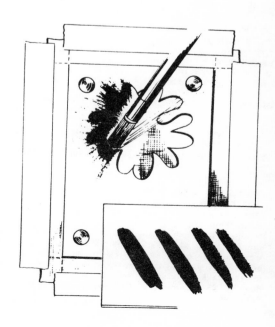

stencil for leaf and stem

1. TRACING DESIGN ON STENCIL PAPER. A separate stencil is cut for each color of the design. Place the translucent stencil paper over the printed pattern and the design will show through. Here, the yellow part of the design is being traced on the stencil paper.

3. SEPARATE STENCILS. This is the cut stencil for the green part of the design. The stencil card for each color of the design must be exactly the same size as all the others. This is necessary because they must be placed accurately on register marks so that the colors will be stenciled in the right spots.

2. CUTTING STENCIL. When the outlines for one color have been traced, place the stencil paper on a block of wood or a very heavy piece of cardboard, and cut along the marked outline with a sharp stencil knife. Then lift out the portion inside the outline. Keep edges sharp and clean.

4. PREPARING TO STEN-CIL. Make register marks with thread or chalk. Place white blotting paper under the fabric, and then stretch it on a board securing it with tape or thumbtacks. Place stencil on register marks and thumbtack it in place.

5. STENCILING. Mix the paint and make a test on a scrap of fabric to be sure the consistency is right. Stroke the brush on a piece of cardboard to remove excess paint as shown. The sweep of the stencil stroke should be from the edge of the stencil opening toward the center so that the paint will not run under. Shading also may be stroked in by working from the stencil edges. The paint must dry before another stencil is placed over it for the next color. Clean stencils carefully.

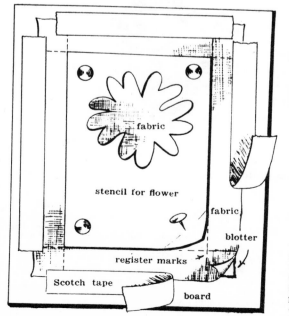

fabric

stencil for flower

fabric

blotter

register marks

Scotch tape

board

TABLECLOTH AT RIGHT. This tablecloth is made of four squares of muslin stitched together. The seam lines are accented with borders of red roses and green leaves stenciled with the designs on Page 22.

CHAIRS AT RIGHT. The rose stencil design on Page 22 may be used for furniture as well as fabric. Natural colors may be used or the design may be stenciled in gold by following the gold stenciling method described in Book 1.

OPPOSITE PAGE, LOWER LEFT. The daisy stencil design on Page 19 is used here in several different ways. The method of painting a background around a white daisy on white fabric is shown here. The white daisies on the opposite page are used in stripes at the ends of a luncheon mat and for a corner motif on a matching napkin. The yellow daisy also is used for a luncheon mat with a green stripe at each end. The daisies are repeated in a scattered informal manner over the entire mat. The same idea could be used for a luncheon cloth of any size, or repeats of daisies could be used with a monogram for sheets, towels or other household linens.

OPPOSITE PAGE, UPPER LEFT. Here, a stenciled monogram is used with flowers and a plain painted border for a guest towel. The design also may be used for sheets by adding more of the small flowers. This zinnia design may be traced directly from the color page onto transparent tracing paper to use either for a painting pattern or a stencil pattern. If the stencil method is used, cut separate stencils for each of the large flowers and one for all of the leaves. Stencil the leaves first. When they are dry, stencil the flowers. The outlining for the pink flower and the leaves may be done with a fine brush or a speed-ball pen after the stenciling is finished. Cut one stencil for each of the three sizes of the small flowers. These may be scattered informally as here or they may make a border or an all-over design. The monogram is stenciled by combining letters in the stencil alphabet on Page 42.

OPPOSITE PAGE, RIGHT. The best parts of old sheets may be used for draperies, bedspreads, dressing table skirts and many other things if they are generously splashed with bold designs in color. This can be a quick and easy job if a large stencil design is repeated at points where it will make the best showing. That is the best part about stenciling—the design may be suited to the way that the material is to be cut. Here the rhododendron design on Page 64 was used. A separate stencil was cut for the light and for the dark parts of the leaves, and one for the pink part of the flowers. The stamens of the flowers are added in black or very dark red with a speed-ball pen.

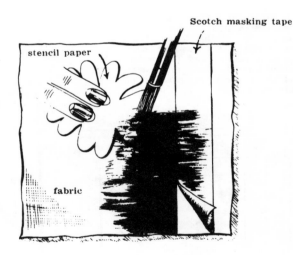

Scotch masking tape

stencil paper

fabric

STRIPES AND PAINTED BACKGROUNDS. The white daisies on the opposite page have a painted blue background which forms a stripe along the ends of the luncheon mat and a square in the corner of the napkin as well as a stripe all the way around it. Straight edges for stripes and other painted areas are obtained by using Scotch masking tape as shown above. When the paint is dry and the tape is pulled away it leaves the edge sharp and clean. When painting a background around a flower motif, cut the flower out of stencil paper, and hold it firmly on the white cloth while the background is being painted as shown here. Use a stiff brush and keep the strokes sweeping outward so that the paint will not go under the stencil paper. Stems, leaves and centers may be stenciled or painted after the background is dry.

ROSE STENCIL DESIGNS. It is easy to cut stencils of these rose motifs, and they may be combined in a number of different ways to stencil a variety of things. The broken lines here and on the opposite page show how they fit together. The rose above may be repeated for a border as for the curtains on the opposite page. It is the central motif in the sheet and pillowcase design. On Page 20, it is used as the central motif for chair backs and a corner motif for the luncheon cloth. It is also effective when repeated as an all-over design for fabric or for decorating walls.

DESIGN ON OPPOSITE PAGE. Cut separate stencils for the flower parts of this design and the parts that are to be stenciled green. The rosebud is stenciled in two tones of pink. The bluebells are a light blue with slightly darker blue shading. A light leaf green should be used for the rest of the design with darker green veins added for rose leaves.

COLORS TO USE FOR THE ROSE DESIGN. It is possible to get variety by using different colors for these roses. They may be red, pink or yellow. A shaded effect may be obtained, as shown here, by brushing a deeper tone on while the stencil is still in place and the light paint is still wet. A pretty two-toned effect is obtained by shading yellow roses with pink. Use a rather light leaf green for the leaves and add veins in a darker green with a fine brush or speed-ball pen. Stems may be the light green shaded a little with brownish green.

BLUEBELLS AND ROSES. The sheet in this sketch is stenciled in pink and blue with the rose at the upper right of the opposite page in the center, the bluebells on this page, and the rose and bud on the opposite page are used at each side of it. The end roses are omitted for the pillowcase.

LEFT. . This plant holder is really a tin can decorated with the small birds on this page. These little songsters are a versatile pair. By adding more of the scroll leaves they may be made into a wide border or an all-over design or they may be used separately for decorating boxes or the corners of napkins or they may be used with a monogram for towels. Paint them in tones of blue, green and yellow, or in blue, yellow and red.

GIFTS AND HOME FURNISHINGS

Gifts may be divided into two classes—the important, impressive type and the small, appealing token. The former are needed for weddings, Christmas and anniversaries. The small token type should be kept in supply for it is better to be forehanded than to miss springing a little surprise at the right moment.

If you become really proficient at painting, your wedding present problem is solved no matter how long your list of marrying friends and relatives. Trays, lamps, book ends, luncheon sets, flower-decked and monogrammed household linens and all the major and minor accessories for the home shown in this book will be stand-outs among any bride's gifts and will please home lovers at any time.

Painted containers of various sorts are favorite gifts for anyone of any age. A young girl will love painted bottles and boxes for her dressing table. Glass containers are pretty and practical for a baby's lotions. Boxes and jars of permanent value may hold hostess gifts of jam, jelly, cake or cookies. On Page 86 of Book 1 there are directions for converting cans into boxes that will give you many ideas along this line. Useful suggestions for painting glass may be found on Page 41 of this book.

It is no oversight that a painted tie rack is not offered here as a man's gift. Why not try something different? Paint a box and fill it with his favorite cigarettes, tobacco or candy. The owl wastebasket on Page 62 was especially designed for a man's study.

OPPOSITE PAGE. The two large garden flower designs are especially planned for stencil patterns. Cut separate stencils for the light and the dark green, also for the red and the blue spire-shaped flowers. When these large masses have been stenciled, petals and details may be added with a fine brush or a speed-ball pen. This is a quick way to decorate a set of small trays or to make all-over repeats for walls or fabrics. The two small flower motifs may be used here and there with the large bouquet or the border or they may be used separately for napkins or small all-over designs. Turn them different ways for variety. The long borders at the sides of the page are useful in decorating tinware. The cock may be used for cocktail napkins or glasses or just for his own decorative design and coloring on most any object of fabric, tin, glass, pottery or wood.

STENCIL A CHRISTMAS TABLECLOTH. If your family enjoys special little Christmas ceremonies each year, here is a new one to add. Stencil a Christmas tablecloth, and keep it to be brought out only for Christmas dinner or perhaps a buffet party during Christmas week. Each year it will bring new pleasure plus the memories of other years until it becomes a family tradition well worth your time and effort. Percale sheeting is used for the cloth shown here. It may be purchased by the yard in a variety of widths so that you may make a cloth any size. If you wish to duplicate the other table decorations shown here, a pattern for the angelic little choir boys and girls is given on Pages 28 and 29. Blocks of wood with holes bored in them hold the candles.

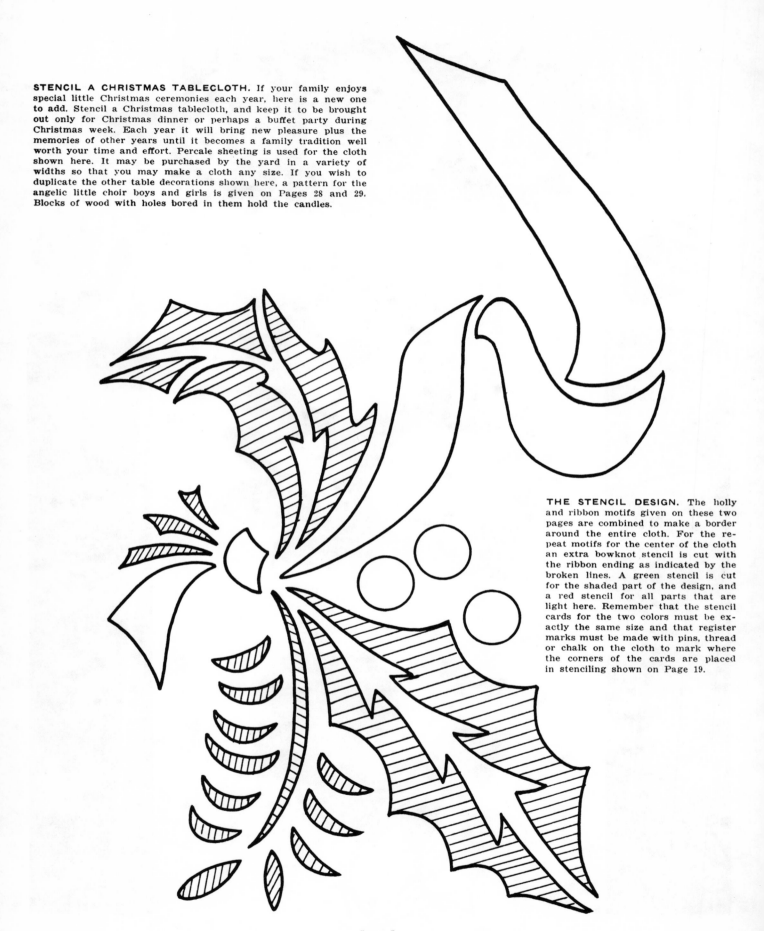

THE STENCIL DESIGN. The holly and ribbon motifs given on these two pages are combined to make a border around the entire cloth. For the repeat motifs for the center of the cloth an extra bowknot stencil is cut with the ribbon ending as indicated by the broken lines. A green stencil is cut for the shaded part of the design, and a red stencil for all parts that are light here. Remember that the stencil cards for the two colors must be exactly the same size and that register marks must be made with pins, thread or chalk on the cloth to mark where the corners of the cards are placed in stenciling shown on Page 19.

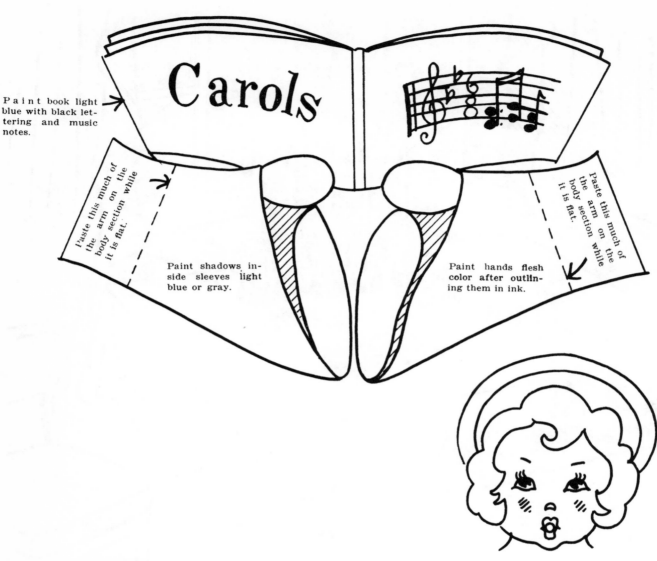

Paint book light blue with black lettering and music notes.

Paste this much of the arm on the body section while it is flat.

Paint shadows inside sleeves light blue or gray.

Paint hands flesh color after outlining them in ink.

Paste this much of the arm on the body section while it is flat.

ANGELS FOR CHRISTMAS DECORATIONS. If you would like to make a set of angelic choir boys and girls that have sprouted wings, here are the patterns and directions for tracing, painting, bending and pasting all the parts so that the figures will stand alone and hold their songbooks in very realistic fashion. The patterns for robe, arms and songbook, and wings are the same for boys and girls. Just substitute the girl's head on this page for that of the boy on the opposite page if you want a mixed choir.

MATERIALS. Stiff drawing paper that will take both ink and watercolor will be needed. Two-ply, kid-finish Bristol board is best. Jet black, waterproof India ink is necessary for outlining, for lettering on song books, and for painting robes and ties. Transparent watercolors are better to use than the opaque type as they do not cover the outlining. Watercolor brushes and a fine pen will be needed, also a good quality of library paste.

HOW TO PAINT THE FACES. When the parts of the figure have been traced and cut out, go over the outlines with a fine pen and waterproof India ink. When this is dry, tint the flesh being careful not to cover the whites of the eyes. Tint the cheeks while the flesh tone is still damp. When the flesh is dry paint mouth, nose and inside of ears red. Paint halo light yellow and eyes and hair whatever color you wish to give a lifelike effect. When mixing the flesh tint, avoid making it too pink. Five parts yellow to one part red thinned with enough water to give a natural flesh tone is a good mixture.

[28]

After the arms have been pasted in place, lap the back edges of the body here and paste.

Paste back portion of arms here and hold firmly until the paste is dry.

Paint this part and the tie with India ink. Also outline the collar in ink.

Paste back portion of arms here and hold firmly until the paste is dry.

Paste wings in place last. Bend them back slightly before pasting.

Paste this center part to the figure after the back joining is dry.

Surprise! note inside —

LEFT. This card is really a folder for a note or letter which may be tied in place with red, green or gold ribbon. The holly and pine design is one of the few in this collection in which no black ink is used. The holly leaves should be painted a deep green with darker green veins. The berries are red with white highlights. The pine branches are green brush or pen strokes with dark brown markings through the center. The cones should be painted a rather light brown with dark brown outlining edges and the small segments. A fine brush or a speed-ball pen may be used for the leaf veins and outlining as well as the fine branches.

RIGHT. This card may be painted with pansies outside and the message inside or the painted design may be repeated both places. Here, an extra piece of note paper has been pasted inside of a folder. The idea may be used for an added message for a special occasion or a note to someone who is ill. In painting the pansies, a black outline for edges and centers gives the flowers character but is not needed for leaves. Keep the upper pansy light. All yellow is good for it. Yellow with blue upper petals may then be used for the one at the lower right, and yellow with deep purple for the flower at the left. Light and medium green are used for leaves and stems with dark green for veins.

PANSIES ARE FOR THOUGHTS AND I AM THINKING OF YOU

PAINT YOUR OWN GREETING CARDS

On this and the following pages are greeting card designs that may be adapted in many ways for special occasions and for different people. Some decorative lettering has been used but most of the cards are to be personalized with your own informal lettering or handwriting. When you add to your message some meaningful bit of decoration the card tells the whole story of your wishes and hopes and sentiments.

Two methods of painting cards are outlined in the directions with these designs. A few of the designs call for the use of opaque watercolors to give shaded effects, but most of them are made by going over traced outlines with waterproof ink and then tinting the design with ordinary transparent watercolor. Both methods give striking effects. A complete list of materials required is given on Page 34.

Loads of Good Cheer !

ABOVE. This design may be used for other occasions as well as Christmas. When the train has been traced and the solid black part neatly inked, paint the cab and the shaded part at the top of the cars red, then paint a line of yellow through the engine and cars. Red also may be used for ribbons on boxes and for car wheels. Shade the smoke from black to gray, and paint the steam at the bottom a light bluish gray. Trace and then paint the lettering in red.

RIGHT. The method of painting this conventionalized holly is shown on Page 32. The ribbon may be painted black and red or two shades of red. Shading is needed for it but no black outline.

COLOR PAGE DESIGNS. The cards shown in color on Pages 32 and 33 may be used as tracing patterns. It is easy to duplicate their coloring.

Greetings

MERRY CHRISTMAS

TRIP
TICKET

*Flowers
that won't fade*

*Fruit that
won't spoil*

*Books you
won't read*

*And a
heart full
of good wishes
from*

A BOUQUET
OF GOOD
WISHES

FOR
YOUR
BIRTHDAY

ABOVE. This card may be used for other anniversaries and occasions that call for good wishes. A mixture of cobalt blue and opaque white is used for the shaded bluebells and ribbon. Cobalt also is used for the forget-me-nots and for the shaded part of the bird. The rest of the bird is white except the yellow bill and black part of eye. The daisy is yellow with center darker yellow shaded with red. The rose is painted with red mixed with white grading the shading up to pale pink. The pansy is purple and yellow with black center and rays.

LEFT. A long strip of paper folded like a ticket for an extended tour is fun to send to anyone who is starting on a trip. You will think of many more things to write and illustrate. A combination of ink outline and color may be used for painting the objects suggested here.

MATERIALS FOR PAINTING CARDS. For cards that are to be folded, a single-ply drawing paper that will take both watercolor and ink will be needed. A two-ply, kid-finish paper is best for cards that are not to be folded. Envelopes to fit may be made of the single-ply paper if stock sizes cannot be found. You will need a bottle of jet black waterproof India ink. A box of assorted transparent watercolors such as school children use will save you a good deal of mixing or you can buy tubes of spectrum red, yellow and blue and do your own mixing. For shaded effects, white opaque watercolor may be mixed with transparent colors. For vivid blues it is suggested that a tube or a jar of opaque cobalt be added to your colors. You will need a fine and a medium fine red sable watercolor brush. No. 0 and No. 2 are good selections. A fine pen and a speed-ball pen will be necessary for outlining. These and the usual carbon paper and transparent tracing paper, mixing dishes and soft, clean rags are all the equipment required.

ABOVE. This simple card is easy to paint and there is ample space inside the fold for a personal message or note. The candle motif alone would be attractive to use at the top of Christmas note paper. The candle holder should be outlined in black and then tinted yellow. The candle is painted red and white with a black shadow under the dripping wax. The flame is blue at the base and yellow at the tip. The first letter of the word Greetings is red shaded with black. The rest of the word is written with a pen and India ink.

RIGHT. If you can make and ink an accurate tracing, you will have no difficulty with this jolly design. All of the parts that are solid black here are inked in solid black. The shaded part of the horse and the bridle and reins are red. Outline the boy in India ink. Tint his suit blue leaving blouse, collar, and buttons white. Tint his face and hands and then paint his hair yellow. Outline the streamer and do the lettering in India ink, then tint the streamer blue. Paint the holly red and green.

Christmas cheer to you and yours

OPPOSITE PAGE, TOP. Wall plaques of wood painted in tile designs have decorative possibilities in any room whether they are hung singly or in a group. The design given here in color may be used as a tracing pattern. The painting is done with American vermilion, medium chrome yellow, cobalt blue, medium chrome green and white. A little of the vermilion red and cobalt added to the green make the dark shade. In painting the bands that frame the plaque, masking tape is used to keep the edges sharp. The wood should be sized with clear varnish before the white background is put on. After the decorating is dry the whole piece should be varnished.

OPPOSITE PAGE, LOWER RIGHT. This cigarette box, so sleek and bright and expensive-looking, began life as a corn can. Like most small-size vegetable and fruit cans its future as a painted box was evident to anyone who had followed the painting hobby. Its red lid is made like that of the tuna fish can beside it except that it has a brass drawer pull for a handle. The tracing pattern for the ravenous bird eating red berries is on Page 43. The paints used are the same as for the tile design above.

OPPOSITE PAGE, LOWER LEFT. Believe it or not, this trinket box was once a tuna fish can. The lid is two layers of plywood with a block of wood on top for a handle. One layer fits inside the can and holds the lid firmly in place. A little glue and a screw through the lid and into the handle holds the parts together. The tracing pattern for the design used for this box is given on Page 41. The paints used are the same as for the tile design above. The method of preparing tinware for painting is fully outlined in PAINTING PATTERNS FOR HOME DECORATORS, Book 1.

FOR PET LOVERS. In a collection of greeting cards of more than three generations ago this holly-bedecked kitten was found. His obvious delight over the whole idea of the festive Christmas season is so contagious that you will want to send him along to all friends who love kittens. For dog lovers, the bright little fellow at the right cannot help but strike a responsive cord whether he is their favorite breed or not.

THE KITTEN. It will be simple to reproduce this kitty on your own greeting cards. Trace all the details carefully and ink in all the heavy outlines and solid blacks. A very light wash of gray may be used where the light-line shading appears here on the face. Paint the tongue red. Paint the bow red and black, the bells black and yellow, and the holly red and green with very dark green for the leaf veins.

THE PUPPY. The puppy design is just as easy to do as the kitten. Make a careful tracing and ink in all solid blacks and heavy outlines with your waterproof India ink, then use a wash of very light gray over the parts where the light-line shading appears here. Keep the box white sharply outlined in black. Paint the ribbon red and black and the holly red and green with very dark green for the leaf veins.

PAINTED LAMP AND SHADE. An unusual lamp base may be made by painting a panel of wood and then boxing it in as shown below. The lamp socket is screwed onto a short length of threaded pipe which is covered with brass nipples above the top board of the lamp base. A nut holds it firmly in place on the under side of the board. The wire comes out at the bottom through a hole bored in the back as shown. The front panel of the lamp base is painted to re-semble a white tile with the graceful design on the opposite page painted in blue, greens and red. All the rest of the lamp base except the painted front panel is the natural wood. The pieces are put together with glue and brads. The heads of the brads are countersunk, covered with plastic wood, sandpapered and then the whole base is varnished with clear varnish. The border designs on the opposite page are painted on a plain paper-parchment shade.

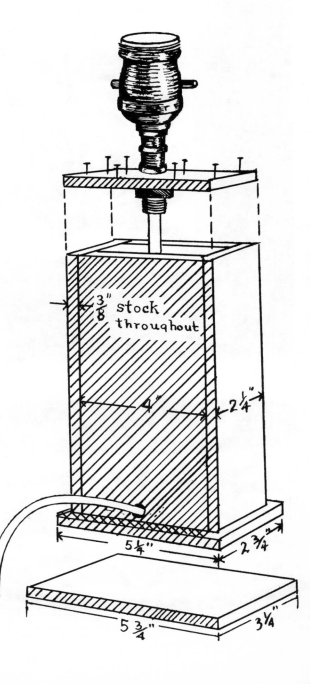

PAINTED WOODEN BOX. The box shown here is made of one-quarter-inch plywood. Sides and ends are joined to bottom with brads and glue. The top is two pieces of the plywood glued together. One of these two plywood layers is cut to fit just inside the box, and holds the lid firmly in place. Joinings were covered with plastic wood. The box was thoroughly sandpapered and given several coats of white paint before the design was painted. Finally an antique glaze was added.

CORNFLOWERS. Cobalt blue. Center of open flowers, chrome yellow with vermilion dots. Calyx and stems of buds, light leaf green. A speed-ball pen may be used for all the stems instead of a fine brush if you do not have a steady hand.

BORDERS. The same coloring is used in the two borders as is outlined here for the rest of the design.

BERRIES. Vermilion with dark brown stems.

BACKGROUND. White or black.

LEAVES. Light parts, light leaf green. Dark parts, bottle green. The leaves should be painted and allowed to dry before the flowers are transferred and painted. A little japan drier mixed with turpentine and varnish as a thinning medium will speed the drying.

DAISIES. White, with yellow centers shaded in vermilion.

TILE DESIGN FOR BOOK ENDS. This pair of book ends is made in the same way that the lamp base on Page 38 is constructed. The front panel is painted on a piece of wood to resemble a square tile. This panel is then boxed in and the book end is finished in the same manner as directed for the lamp base. Before the top is fastened on, the hollow part of the boxlike construction is filled with sand or shot to make the book end heavy. This square boxed-in tile effect is attractive when made into a pair of matching lamp bases with plain squarish shades in one of the bright colors in the painted design. Such a pair of lamps, one at each side of a mirror, gives dignity to a chest of drawers in the hall, living room or dining room.

BACKGROUND. White is best ot give the effect of a tile. A glaze of clear varnish after the painted design is dry will heighten this effect.

LEAVES. Shaded part of leaves and the stems, bottle green. Light parts of leaves, light leaf green. Here again, a speed-ball pen may be used for stems instead of a fine brush if this part of the design seems difficult.

Part of flower shaded in straight lines, vermilion. Part shaded with crossed lines, dark red. All of the light parts, medium chrome yellow.

Center dot, medium chrome yellow shaded with the vermilion. Other dots circling this center are cobalt blue.

The two crescent shaped sections, vermilion. Dot, medium chrome yellow.

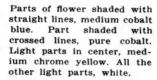

Parts of flower shaded with straight lines, medium cobalt blue. Part shaded with crossed lines, pure cobalt. Light parts in center, medium chrome yellow. All the other light parts, white.

Part of bud shaded in straight lines, rose pink. Part with crossed lines, American vermilion. The part shown in black here is painted bottle green. The light rays around the flower, light leaf green.

This bud and the smaller one like it, shaded in straight lines, American vermilion. Lightest parts, white. Darkest parts, dark red.

Medium chrome yellow with red shading.

Inner circle of center, medium chrome yellow. Outer circle of center, white with red dots. Petals cobalt blue with white dots.

Shaded petals, American vermilion. Center petal and two rays at tip, the medium chrome yellow. Calyx and base of flower, light leaf green.

Inner circle of center, medium chrome yellow. Outer circle, white with light leaf green dots. Round part of petals, cobalt blue with straight base portions of petals dark blue. The large and the small berry near this flower are the chrome yellow shaded with red.

PAINTING ON GLASS. It is possible to buy special paint for decorating glass at art supply stores. Ordinary tube oil colors mixed with clear varnish and a little Japan drier also adhere well, and may be used a long time without wearing off.

MOSS ROSE DESIGN. This flower motif appears again and again in the folk arts of Czechoslovakia. It has been adapted from colorful embroideries for the painting patterns in this book. A large tracing pattern of it is given above. Another is given in color on Page 45. The design on the glass box at the right appears in another size in the front of the book. Any of these may be used as tracing patterns, and the version in color may be followed as a painting guide.

GLASS BOTTLE AND POWDER BOX. Decorated bottles and glass containers lend color and sparkle to a dressing table or bathroom shelf. The glittering top for the bottle above is a glass drawer pull fastened to the plastic top of a medicine bottle by boring a hole in the plastic for the metal bolt attached to the knob. A matching handle is used for the glass powder box at the left which was once a glass jar for smoked tongue. The box lid is made of plywood.

SALT AND PEPPERS. If you would like to own a set of green glass salt and pepper shakers decorated in gay flowers, save the small colored glass bottles with plastic tops that so many druggists use now. Holes may be bored in the tops with a needle-point drill. Tiny decorating designs may be traced right from the sketches at the left or the larger patterns on Page 44 may be used. The designs appear in color on Page 45.

A PAINTED MUSTARD JAR. Sandwiches and party snacks always call for mustard. So dress up an ordinary mustard jar with bright painted flowers on sides and top and bands of dark green to accent the molded shape of the glass. The design used for the jar at the right is an adaptation of the tile design shown in color on Page 37. The flowers in the colored sketch may be used for tracing patterns and color guides.

[41]

ABCDEFGHIJ
KLMNOPQRS
TUVWXYZ

STENCILED MONOGRAMS. Both wearing apparel and household linens may be monogrammed with these smart, slim letters. Try a two or a three-letter monogram at the bottom of a man's tie or on a scarf or a sports shirt or a dress. Your best towels and sheets may be monogrammed in a few minutes by this method. Any of the small flower or bird designs in this book may be combined with the letters. An especially attractive combination with flowers to be used for a towel or to decorate the top of a sheet is shown in color on Page 21. Good effects also may be obtained with simple arrangements of the letters without decoration or by stenciling them in different colors as shown here.

HOW TO USE THESE LETTERS. In the stencil alphabet above, breaks in the letters form little bridges so that the letters will hold together when cut out of stencil paper. After the letters have been stenciled on the fabric these breaks may be filled in with the fabric paint and a fine brush to make solid letters like those shown in the monograms at the left. When preparing the stencil trace the letters on the stencil paper and cut them out in the same manner as shown for the flower on Page 19. If more than one color is to be used or if you want to arrange the letters in different ways for decorating different things, cut a separate stencil for each letter of the monogram. Once the stencil is cut, it may be used over and over.

CAUTION. When working **with** textile paint use thinner sparingly. Too much will cause colors to run. Test the paint mixture on the same fabric you are going to paint before you start the work. In stenciling be sure one color is dry before another stencil is placed over it. Clean stencils with a soft cloth and a little brush cleaner. In this way smudges will be avoided and the stencils may be used over and over.

ABOVE. This design may be used for the tin tops of glass jars or it may be painted on the under side of a round glass ash tray. In decorating a glass dish in this way the colors show through but are not marred by use. Paint the rose pink and white. Use two shades of green for foliage. Paint the smallest flower bright blue and the center flower yellow.

RIGHT. These are the tracing patterns for the designs shown in color for the pair of boxes on Page 37. They may have many other uses. The bird design is especially good for a small rectangular tray. The usual American vermilion, medium chrome yellow, cobalt blue, medium chrome green and white are the basic colors used in painting all of these 'designs.

LEFT, THE COVER DESIGN. This is the tracing pattern for the flowers shown in color on the cover of this book. Parts or all of the pattern may have many variations and dozens of different applications. The beautiful orange color used for the background on the cover may be mixed by following the formula for Burnt Orange in Book 1. Or try the design on a black background for a tray, or a white ground for a luncheon set, or on white or cream on natural wood for decorating a salt box or a chest of drawers. If one of these more neutral backgrounds is used, red or orange should be substituted for the white in the design on the cover. The whole pattern or separate flowers may be turned in various ways in making repeats for borders and all-over designs to fit different spaces.

ABOVE, EARLY AMERICAN TRAY DESIGN. The tracing pattern and color guide for this design are on Pages 10 and 11. The color effect obtained with this type of brush-stroke painting is illustrated at the lower right of the opposite page. The strokes are sharply defined here so that their sweep will be clear. Actually, when working with wet oil paint, they blend slightly giving softer color gradation.

OPPOSITE PAGE, TOP. These panels show the front and top of a decorated box. The designs may be traced directly from these color sketches which also will serve as a painting guide. The center part of the front panel design may be used for the ends of the box.

OPPOSITE PAGE, LEFT. Tracing patterns for glass containers with plastic tops are given on this page and in a smaller size on Page 41. The design for the glass dish with wooden lid and glass handle also is given on Page 41 and in a larger size in the front of this book. The design at the top of this page is suitable for larger glass containers.

A STENCILED APRON. One way to a man's heart is to give him an apron that is not all flounces and frills and dainty dimity. A butchers' type of apron may be made of heavy muslin and decorated with a stenciled design of this expert chef. Cut one stencil for the light blue shirt and one for the dark blue trousers, then cut a third stencil for the shoes and black outlines.

KITCHEN DECORATIONS

The motto over the stove is the keynote of this kitchen. Hearts in bold red brush strokes, with favorite recipes in the centers repeat the theme around the room. Rules for gravies and sauces and cooking times for meats are in the hearts near the stove. Salads are over the sink, pastry recipes near the mixing center.

The Swedish rose design on Page 49 frames the clock as well as some of the hearts. Where hearts are used on cupboard doors, motifs from Page 50 are added to fill the space attractively. The design on Page 51, with extra roses added at the top, is used for lower cupboard doors. Other motifs from Page 50 are used for drawer fronts, canisters, knife box,

breadboard, breadbox, chair and other things in the room. The tiniest roses are used for spice jars lined up on a narrow shelf over the stove. This set is made from small mayonnaise jars with holes drilled in the lids with a needle-point drill.

The motto over the stove was drawn out on a piece of wrapping paper first by following the script alphabet given in PAINTING PATTERNS FOR HOME DECORATORS, Book 1. It was then traced on the wall and painted in an informal manner in red. The lettering directions in Book 1 also were followed with good results in marking the spice set and other containers.

YOUR FAVORITE RECIPES

Outline hearts with bold strokes on kitchen walls or cupboard doors, then cut out recipes and paste them in the centers of the hearts. In this way basic or foundation recipes are always in sight when needed. If rubber cement is used to paste the recipe in place, it may be peeled off easily when you want a change. Here, flowers and a bowknot are used to embellish the heart motif. In the sketch on Page 47, unadorned hearts are used below the wall motto while elaborate flower sprays frame those on cupboard doors.

SWEDISH ROSE DESIGN. Since Swedish housewives are famous for their delectable cookery and, since it is traditional with them that the walls of their homes and many articles of everyday use are decorated with hand-painted designs, it seems fitting that a Swedish motif should be chosen for kitchen decorations. This is the pattern for the design that frames the clock on Page 47. The outline for half of a large heart also is given here.

HOW TO PAINT THE DESIGN. Typical Swedish rose and leaf designs are painted in the true free brush-stroke manner. However, a traced outline to follow will give you confidence and need not interfere with the freedom of brush work. The strokes for the leaves and stems are clearly outlined. Use a good medium leaf green and start strokes at the outside edge of the leaf. As the strokes overlap toward the base of the leaf, a shaded effect results. Paint the roses and buds pink first and then, while the pink is still wet, add brush-stroke shading in red as shown here. All of these sketches are planned to show the direction and swirl of the red strokes. The flowers are seemingly much alike and yet quite different. Actually, in painting the roses the wet colors blend slightly giving a much softer effect.

EXTRA ROSES AND SPRAYS. Here are extra Swedish rose motifs to be added to other designs to fill large cupboard door spaces and to use for drawer fronts and for decorating other articles as shown in the sketch on Page 47. The method of painting the roses is outlined on Page 49. They are effective on either a light or a dark background.

USES FOR THIS DESIGN. When used for kitchen decorations this design is usually painted on a white or a light ground. It also makes a beautiful tray design on a black ground. By adding extra flower sprays, it may be used on a black ground to paint a typical Swedish chest to use for blankets.

SWEDISH ROSE AND BOWKNOT DESIGN. This design is painted in the same manner as described on Page 49 except that there are extra sprays of small flowers painted in medium cobalt blue with medium leaf green leaves and stems. The ribbon is painted in two tones of the cobalt blue.

[51]

OTHER USES FOR DUTCH BIRDS. Here is another adaptation of the Dutch bird design. It is used singly here with a frame all its own. The coloring is the same as outlined on Page 8. This design would be good to use for decorating a wastebasket. It also would be exactly right for cupboard doors in a kitchen with Pennsylvania Dutch coloring. If used for a pair of doors, turn the tracing pattern over for one door so that the birds will face each other. Parts of the flower motifs given here and on the title page of this book may be used for other decorations in the room, so that matching designs will be repeated throughout. A small matching border in color is given on Page 25.

NO LOST KEYS. Even the key to a heart may be found here. Trace the shape of the board onto a piece of one-half or three-eighths-inch lumber. Have it cut and a hole bored at the top. Sandpaper it, and then varnish with clear varnish. Transfer the design next, then paint the big key a brassy yellow, the ribbon bright blue with darker shading, the heart red and white, the daisies yellow and orange with red and yellow centers, and the leaves bottle green with yellow veins. Paint the edge of the board red. When dry, screw a brass hook at the base of each flower and then varnish the whole thing with clear varnish.

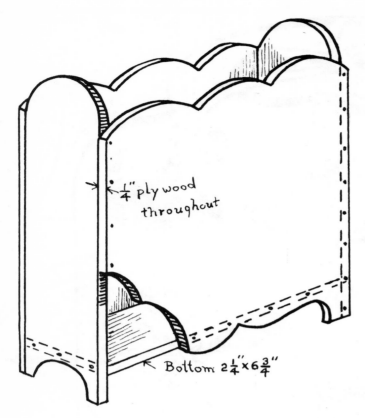

NAPKIN HOLDER. Any breakfast nook will be a brighter spot with this paper napkin holder painted in a gay peasant design. The simple construction with glue and brads is typical of the way boxes and many other things may be made to paint. Joinings should be covered with plastic wood, and sanded thoroughly. Two or three coats of enamel with plenty of drying time between coats will then make a perfectly smooth surface on which to trace and paint the design.

$\frac{1}{4}''$ ply wood throughout

Bottom $2\frac{1}{4}'' \times 6\frac{3}{4}''$

END DESIGN. Heart is outlined in American vermilion. Top motif and grasses, as indicated. All the rest of the design, the same as the front.

CUTTING PATTERN. This outline may be used as a pattern for cutting the shaped ends of the napkin holder. The outline enclosing the design below is the exact shape of the front and back. Dimensions for the bottom are given in the diagram on the opposite page.

BACKGROUND. White with a glaze of clear varnish applied after the painted design is dry.

cobalt blue

cobalt blue

vermilion

cobalt blue

FLOWERS. Parts shaded with straight lines, medium cobalt blue. Parts shaded with crossed lines, pure cobalt. Light parts, medium chrome yellow.

LEAVES. Shaded parts, bottle green. Light parts and dots at base of flowers, light leaf green.
BERRIES. Vermilion red.

BRANCH. Twig, medium brown. Leaves, medium chrome green. Berries, vermilion with dark brown tips.

BACKGROUND. Black.

BORDER. Outside, vermilion dots and green dashes. Inside, green leaves and vermilion berries with dark brown tips.

BLUE BIRD. Part shaded with closely spaced straight lines, cobalt blue. Part shaded with crossed lines, cobalt darkened a little with red. Breast, American vermilion with a touch of cobalt, medium chrome yellow and white. Beak, legs, and feet, yellow. Eye, white and brownish black.

BRANCH, BORDER AND BACK-GROUND. Same as outlined on opposite page.

CARDINAL. Part shaded in straight lines, American vermilion. Part shaded in crossed lines, wine red. Around eye, bluish black to contrast slightly with background. Eye, black and white. Beak, legs and feet, medium chrome yellow.

PAIR OF TRAYS. These trays make most satisfactory lap trays for a buffet supper, and are extremely attractive for wall plaques. Actually, they are just pie tins which have risen from their lowly state by means of clever decorations that will set any party buzzing with lively conversation.

[57]

PEACOCK TRAY DESIGN. This design makes a handsome tray with the peacock painted in full color as indicated, and the grapes for background and border stenciled in gold. Or the grape design may be painted if it is kept subdued in color. If a black foundation paint is used, the final finish should be clear white, transparent, waterproof varnish. If a colored ground is used, add raw umber to the varnish for the final finish. Formulas for a number of different antique finishes and overtones are given in Book 1.

BACKGROUND. Black is first choice for background for this design though light lemon yellow or stone gray also are good.

HOW TO PAINT THE PEACOCK. An enlargement of the peacock's tail is given on this page so that the color guide will be easy to follow. The colors for the body are indicated on the opposite page. The outside outlines of the entire bird should be transferred when the background color is dry. The whole bird should then be painted peacock blue and allowed to dry before transferring the details of the design. When this is done, follow the color guides in filling in details with a very fine pointed brush.

GRAPES AND LEAVES. If grapes and leaves for background and border are gold stenciled, the work is done by dipping a piece of velvet into gold powder, and rubbing it through openings in a stencil onto varnish which is just dry enough to be sticky. Black center portions for the leaves are added later with a brush. The whole process, including the cutting of the stencil is explained in detail in Book 1. If it should be decided to paint the grapes and leaves instead of stenciling them, paint the leaves a neutral olive green with darker veins, and the grapes, grape blue shading each one to be a little darker on the left side. Keep this whole part of the design more subdued than the peacock.

Tracing pattern for the tray border.

[58]

LEAVES AND STEMS. The same coloring is used for main design and added sprays. Stems and shaded leaves, bottle green. Light leaves, light leaf green.

HEART. Part shaded with crossed lines, dark red. Part shaded with straight lines, American vermilion. Lightest part, white.

The shaded part of this flower and others like it in the design are painted medium cobalt blue. The light part is white. The dots are yellow.

BACKGROUND. Black or greenish gray make a good ground for this pattern.

Light parts of this pair of flowers, yellow. Shaded part is vermilion red.

cobalt blue

light cobalt

HEART AND FLOWERS. A design similar to this but smaller is shown in full color in Book 1. There have been many requests for a larger version, and here it is. The portion of the design on the opposite page may be used by itself for cupboard doors or for such things as the wastebasket shown on Page 62. When the extra flower sprays on this page are added, the design adequately fills a large oval tray or it may be used for a rectangular tray quite as well. The two harmonizing brush-stroke borders given here may be used with many different designs for trays of various shapes.

HOW TO ADD FLOWER SPRAYS. Trace the design on the opposite page and the sprays on this page on separate pieces of transparent tracing paper. In this way the transparent tracing pattern for the sprays may be turned over to add them to the left side of the main design. It will be necessary to shift the transparent pattern slightly to make the sprays fit between the leaves of the main design, as one of the things that lends interest to a decorating pattern of this informal type is that it is not exactly alike on both sides. If architects' transparent tracing paper is used, a soft pencil outline on the side that is placed face down will transfer easily by tracing over the line with considerable pressure from the side that is up. Carbon paper will not be needed, and you can see where the sprays are being placed.

The light parts of this flower and bud are the y e l l o w. Shaded parts a r e painted vermilion red.

All of the flowers of this shape in the design are painted vermilion with dark red s h a d i n g as shown.

Shaded parts of this flower and the lower buds, cobalt blue. Light parts, yellow.

BORDERS. In decorating antique trays it seems to have been the custom to paint borders of this type lemon yellow with m e d i u m brown shading. Y e l l o w may be used for the outer border and light leaf and bottle green for the inside border.

[61]

OPPOSITE PAGE. In this group the heart and flower pattern on Pages 60 and 61 has been used for a large oval tray and for decorating a metal wastebasket. The owl pattern on this page has been applied to a wastebasket which is easy to make of plywood. Such a basket should be sanded and varnished before the design is applied on the natural wood color.

THE OWL DESIGN. The first step is to trace the outside outlines of the owl and paint the entire bird cream color. Several coats may be needed to cover .the background. When the cream-colored paint is dry, transfer the details of the design to it. The parts of the bird that are solid black here are painted a very dark brown. The parts shaded with diagonal lines, tan. The parts shaded with crossed lines, medium brown. The tree branch is medium and dark brown. The leaves are light and medium leaf green with very dark green veins.

[63]

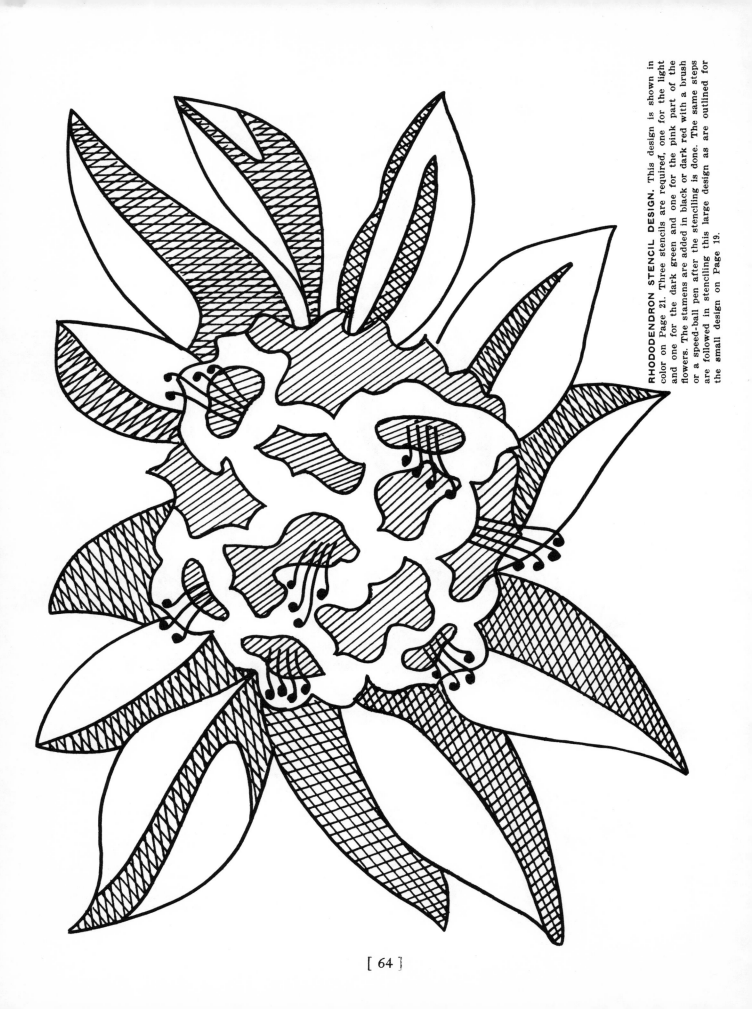

RHODODENDRON STENCIL DESIGN. This design is shown in color on Page 21. Three stencils are required, one for the light and one for the dark green and one for the pink part of the flowers. The stamens are added in black or dark red with a brush or a speed-ball pen after the stenciling is done. The same steps are followed in stenciling this large design as are outlined for the small design on Page 19.